San Diego Padres 2020

A Baseball Companion

Edited by R.J. Anderson, Craig Goldstein and Bret Sayre

Baseball Prospectus

Craig Brown, Steven Goldman and David Pease, Consultant Editors
Robert Au, Harry Pavlidis and Amy Pircher, Statistics Editors

Copyright © 2020 by DIY Baseball, LLC.
All rights reserved

This book or any part thereof may not be reproduced or transmitted in any form or by any means, electronic or mechanical, including photocopying, recording, or by any information storage and retrieval system, without permission in writing from the publisher.

Limit of Liability/Disclaimer of Warranty: While the publisher and the author have used their best efforts in preparing this book, they make no representations or warranties with respect to the accuracy or completeness of the contents of this book and specifically disclaim any implied warranties of merchantability or fitness for a particular purpose. No warranty may be created or extended by sales representatives or written sales materials. The advice and strategies contained herein may not be suitable for your situation. You should consult with a professional where appropriate. Neither the publisher nor the author shall be liable for any loss of profit or any other commercial damages, including but not limited to special, incidental, consequential, or other damages.

Library of Congress Cataloging-in-Publication Data:
paperback
ISBN-13: 978-1-950716-16-6

Project Credits
Cover Design: Michael Byzewski at Aesthetic Apparatus
Interior Design and Production: Jeff Pease, Dave Pease
Layout: Jeff Pease, Dave Pease

Baseball icon courtesy of Uberux, from https://www.shareicon.net/author/uberux

Ballpark diagram courtesy of Lou Spirito/THIRTY81 Project, https://thirty81project.com/

Manufactured in the United States of America
10 9 8 7 6 5 4 3 2 1

Table of Contents

Statistical Introduction v

Part 1: Team Analysis

San Diego Padres: Where Are You Going, Where Have You Been? 3
  Jarrett Seidler, Wilson Karaman and Matthew Trueblood

Performance Graphs 7

2019 Team Performance 8

2020 Team Projections 9

Team Personnel 10

Petco Park Stats 11

Padres Team Analysis 13

Part 2: Player Analysis

Padres Player Analysis 20

Padres Prospects 101

Part 3: Featured Articles

The Baseball Is Juiced (Again) 119
  Robert Arthur

The Moral Hazard of Playing It Safe 123
  Craig Goldstein

Index of Names 129

Statistical Introduction

Sports are, fundamentally, a blend of athletic endeavor and storytelling. Baseball, like any other sport, tells its stories in so many ways: in the arc of a game from the stands or a season from the box scores, in photos, or even in numbers. At Baseball Prospectus, we understand that statistics don't replace observation or any of baseball's stories, but complement everything else that makes the game so much fun.

What stats help us with is with patterns and precision, variance and value. This book can help you learn things you may not see from watching a game or hundred, whether it's the path of a career over time or the breadth of the entire MLB. We'd also never ask you to choose between our numbers and the experience of viewing a game from the cheap seats or the comfort of your home; our publication combines running the numbers with observations and wisdom from some of the brightest minds we can find. But if you *do* want to learn more about the numbers beyond what's on the backs of player jerseys, let us help explain.

Offense

We've revised our methodology for determining batting value. Long-time readers of the book will notice that we've retired True Average in favor of a new metric: Deserved Runs Created Plus (DRC+). Developed by Jonathan Judge and our stats team, this statistic measures everything a player does at the plate–reaching base, hitting for power, making outs, and moving runners over–and puts it on a scale where 100 equals league-average performance. A DRC+ of 150 is terrific, a DRC+ of 100 is average and a DRC+ of 75 means you better be an excellent defender.

DRC+ also does a better job than any of our previous metrics in taking contextual factors into account. The model adjusts for how the park affects performance, but also for things like the talent of the opposing pitcher, value of different types of batted-ball events, league, temperature and other factors. It's able to describe a player's expected offensive contribution than any other statistic we've found over the years, and also does a better job of predicting future performance as well.

There's a lot more to DRC+'s story, and you can read all about it in greater depth near the end of this book.

The other aspect of run-scoring is baserunning, which we quantify using Baserunning Runs. BRR not only records the value of stolen bases (or getting caught in the act), but also accounts for all the stuff that doesn't show up on the back of a baseball card: a runner's ability to go first to third on a single, or advance on a fly ball.

Defense

Where offensive value is *relatively* easy to identify and understand, defensive value is...not. Over the past dozen years, the sabermetric community has focused mostly on stats based on zone data: a real-live human person records the type of batted ball and estimated landing location, and models are created that give expected outs. From there, you can compare fielders' actual outs to those expected ones. Simple, right?

Unfortunately, zone data has two major issues. First, zone data is recorded by commercial data providers who keep the raw data private unless you pay for it. (All the statistics we build in this book and on our website use public data as inputs.) That hurts our ability to test assumptions or duplicate results. Second, over the years it has become apparent that there's quite a bit of "noise" in zone-based fielding analysis. Sometimes the conclusions drawn from zone data don't hold up to scrutiny, and sometimes the different data provided by different providers don't look anything alike, giving wildly different results. Sometimes the hard-working professional stringers or scorers might unknowingly inflict unconscious bias into the mix: for example good fielders will often be credited with more expected outs despite the data, and ballparks with high press boxes tend to score more line drives than ones with a lower press box.

Enter our Fielding Runs Above Average (FRAA). For most positions, FRAA is built from play-by-play data, which allows us to avoid the subjectivity found in many other fielding metrics. The idea is this: count how many fielding plays are made by a given player and compare that to expected plays for an average fielder at their position (based on pitcher ground ball tendencies and batter handedness). Then we adjust for park and base-out situations.

When it comes to catchers, our methodology is a little different thanks to the laundry list of responsibilities they're tasked with beyond just, well, catching and throwing the ball. By now you've probably heard about "framing" or the art of making umpires more likely to call balls outside the strike zone for strikes. To put this into one tidy number, we incorporate pitch tracking data (for the years it exists) and adjust for important factors like pitcher, umpire, batter and home-field advantage using a mixed-model approach. This grants us a number for how many strikes the catcher is personally adding to (or subtracting from) his pitchers' performance...which we then convert to runs added or lost using linear weights.

Framing is one of the biggest parts of determining catcher value, but we also take into account blocking balls from going past, whether a scorer deems it a passed ball or a wild pitch. We use a similar approach—one that really benefits from the pitch tracking data that tells us what ends up in the dirt and what doesn't. We also include a catcher's ability to prevent stolen bases and how well they field balls in play, and *finally* we come up with our FRAA for catchers.

Pitching

Both pitching and fielding make up the half of baseball that isn't run scoring: run prevention. Separating pitching from fielding is a tough task, and most recent pitching analysis has branched off from Voros McCracken's famous (and controversial) statement, "There is little if any difference among major-league pitchers in their ability to prevent hits on balls hit in the field of play." The research of the analytic community has validated this to some extent, and there are a host of "defense-independent" pitching measures that have been developed to try and extract the effect of the defense behind a hurler from the pitcher's work.

Our solution to this quandary is Deserved Run Average (DRA), our core pitching metric. DRA looks like earned run average (ERA), the tried-and-true pitching stat you've seen on every baseball broadcast or box score from the past century, but it's very different. To start, DRA takes an event-by-event look at what the pitchers does, and adjusts the value of that event based on different environmental factors like park, batter, catcher, umpire, base-out situation, run differential, inning, defense, home field advantage, pitcher role and temperature. That mixed model gives us a pitcher's expected contribution, similar to what we do for our DRC+ model for hitters and FRAA model for catchers. (Oh, and we also consider the pitcher's effect on basestealing and on balls getting past the catcher.)

It's important to note that DRA is set to the scale of runs allowed per nine innings (RA9) instead of ERA, which makes DRA's scale slightly higher than ERA's. The reason for this is because ERA tends to overrate three types of pitchers:

1. Pitchers who play in parks where scorers hand out more errors. Official scorers differ significantly in the frequency at which they assign errors to fielders.
2. Ground-ball pitchers, because a substantial proportion of errors occur on groundballs.
3. Pitchers who aren't very good. Better pitchers often allow fewer unearned runs than bad pitchers, because good pitchers tend to find ways to get out of jams.

Since the last time you picked up an edition of this book, we've also made a few minor changes to DRA to make it better. Recent research into "tunneling"—the act of throwing consecutive pitches that appear similar from a batter's point of view until after the swing decision point–data has given us a new contextual factor to account for in DRA: plate distance. This refers to the distance between successive pitches as they approach the plate, and while it has a smaller effect than factors like velocity or whiff rate, it still can help explain pitcher strikeout rate in our model.

New Pitching Metrics for 2020

We're including a few "new" pitching metrics in the book for the 2020 edition, though unlike last year, these numbers may be a little bit more familiar to those of you who have spent some time investigating baseball statistics.

Fastball Percentage

Our fastball percentage (FB%) statistic measures how frequently a pitcher throws a pitch classified as a "fastball," measured as a percentage of overall pitches thrown. We qualify three types of fastballs:

1. The traditional four-seam fastball;
2. The two-seam fastball or sinker;
3. "Hard cutters," which are pitches that have the movement profile of a cut fastball and are used as the pitcher's primary offering or in place of a more traditional fastball.

For example, a pitcher with a FB% of 67 throws any combination of these three pitches about two-thirds of the time.

Whiff Rate

Everybody loves a swing and a miss, and whiff rate (WHF) measures how frequently pitchers induce a swinging strike. To calculate WHF, we add up all the pitches thrown that ended with a swinging strike, then divide that number by a pitcher's total pitches thrown. Most often, high whiff rates correlate with high strikeout rates (and overall effective pitcher performance).

Called Strike Probability

Called Strike Probability (CSP) is a number that represents the likelihood that all of a pitcher's pitches will be called a strike while controlling for location, pitcher and batter handedness, umpire and count. Here's how it works: on each pitch, our model determines how many times (out of 100) that a similar pitch was called for a strike given those factors mentioned above, and when normalized for each batter's strike zone. Then we average the CSP for all pitches thrown by a pitcher in a season, and that gives us the yearly CSP percentage you see in the stats boxes.

As you might imagine, pitchers with a higher CSP are more likely to work in the zone, where pitchers with a lower CSP are likely locating their pitches outside the normal strike zone, for better or for worse.

Projections

Many of you aren't turning to this book just for a look at what a player has done, but for a look at what a player is going to do: the PECOTA projections. PECOTA, initially developed by Nate Silver (who has moved on to greater fame as a political analyst), consists of three parts:

1. Major-league equivalencies, which use minor-league statistics to project how a player will perform in the major leagues;
2. Baseline forecasts, which use weighted averages and regression to the mean to estimate a player's current true talent level; and
3. Aging curves, which uses the career paths of comparable players to estimate how a player's statistics are likely to change over time.

With all those important things covered, let's take a look at what's in the book this year.

Team Prospectus

Most of this book is composed of team chapters, with one for each of the 30 major-league franchises. On the first page of each chapter, you'll see a box that contains some of the key statistics for each team as well as a very inviting stadium diagram. (You can see an example of this for the Milwaukee Brewers on this very page!)

We start with the team name, their unadjusted 2019 win-loss record, and their divisional ranking. Beneath that are a host of other team statistics. **Pythag** presents an adjusted 2019 winning percentage, calculated by taking runs scored per game (**RS/G**) and runs allowed per game (**RA/G**) for the team, and running them through a version of Bill James' Pythagorean formula that was refined and improved by David Smyth and Brandon Heipp. (The formula is called "Pythagenpat," which is equally fun to type and to say.)

Next up is **DRC+**, described earlier, to indicate the overall hitting ability of the team either above or below league-average. Run prevention on the pitching side is covered by **DRA** (also mentioned earlier) and another metric: Fielding Independent Pitching (**FIP**), which calculates another ERA-like statistic based on strikeouts, walks, and home runs recorded. Defensive Efficiency Rating (**DER**) tells us the percentage of balls in play turned into outs for the team, and is a quick fielding shorthand that rounds out run prevention.

After that, we have several measures related to roster composition, as opposed to on-field performance. **B-Age** and **P-Age** tell us the average age of a team's batters and pitchers, respectively. **Salary** is the combined team payroll for all on-field players, and Doug Pappas' Marginal Dollars per Marginal Win (**M$/MW**) tells us how much money a team spent to earn production above replacement level.

Ending this batch of statistics is the number of disabled list days a team had over the season (**IL Days**) and the amount of salary paid to players on the disabled list (**$ on IL**); this final number is expressed as a percentage of total payroll.

Next to each of these stats, we've listed each team's MLB rank in that category from first to 30th. In this, first always indicates a positive outcome and 30th a negative outcome, except in the case of salary—first is highest.

After the franchise statistics, we share a few items about the team's home ballpark. There's the aforementioned diagram of the park's dimensions (including distances to the outfield wall), a graphic showing the height of the wall from the left-field pole to the right-field pole, and a table showing three-year park factors for the stadium. The park factors are displayed as indexes where 100 is average, 110 means that the park inflates the statistic in question by 10 percent, and 90 means that the park deflates the statistic in question by 10 percent.

On the second page of each team chapter, you'll find three graphs. The first is the **2019 Hit List Ranking**. This shows our Hit List Rank for the team on each day of the 2019 season and is intended to give you a picture of the ups and downs of the team's season. Hit List Rank measures overall team performance and drives the Hit List Power Rankings at the baseballprospectus.com website.

The second graph is **Committed Payroll** and helps you see how the team's payroll has compared to the MLB and divisional average payrolls over time. Payroll figures are current as of January 1, 2020; with so many free agents still unsigned as of this writing, the final 2020 figure will likely be significantly different for many teams. (In the meantime, you can always find the most current data at Baseball Prospectus' Cot's Baseball Contracts page.)

The third graph is **Farm System Ranking** and displays how the Baseball Prospectus prospect team has ranked the organization's farm system since 2007.

After the graphs, we have a **Personnel** section that lists many of the important decision-makers and upper-level field and operations staff members for the franchise, as well as any former Baseball Prospectus staff members who are currently part of the organization. (In very rare circumstances, someone might be on both lists!)

Juan Soto LF
Born: 10/25/98 Age: 21 Bats: L Throws: L
Height: 6'1" Weight: 185 Origin: International Free Agent, 2015

YEAR	TEAM	LVL	AGE	PA	R	2B	3B	HR	RBI	BB	K	SB	CS	AVG/OBP/SLG
2017	NAT	RK	18	27	3	1	1	0	4	2	1	0	0	.320/.370/.440
2017	HAG	A	18	96	15	5	0	3	14	10	8	1	2	.360/.427/.523
2018	HAG	A	19	74	12	5	3	5	24	14	13	2	0	.373/.486/.814
2018	POT	A+	19	73	17	3	1	7	18	11	8	0	1	.371/.466/.790
2018	HAR	AA	19	35	4	2	0	2	10	4	7	1	0	.323/.400/.581
2018	WAS	MLB	19	494	77	25	1	22	70	79	99	5	2	.292/.406/.517
2019	WAS	MLB	20	659	110	32	5	34	110	108	132	12	1	.282/.401/.548
2020	WAS	MLB	21	630	92	30	3	35	102	85	123	5	2	.284/.382/.543

Comparables: Ronald Acuña Jr., Mike Trout, Tony Conigliaro

YEAR	TEAM	LVL	AGE	PA	DRC+	VORP	BABIP	BRR	FRAA	WARP
2017	NAT	RK	18	27	135	1.5	.333	0.0	RF(9): -1.1	0.0
2017	HAG	A	18	96	181	8.0	.373	1.0	RF(19): -1.9, LF(2): -0.3	0.9
2018	HAG	A	19	74	222	14.5	.405	0.3	RF(14): 1.1, CF(2): 0.2	1.2
2018	POT	A+	19	73	260	15.4	.340	1.4	RF(14): 1.0, LF(1): 0.0	1.6
2018	HAR	AA	19	35	113	3.6	.364	0.0	LF(4): 0.6, RF(4): -0.5	0.1
2018	WAS	MLB	19	494	125	40.5	.338	-0.5	LF(114): 2.7	3.0
2019	WAS	MLB	20	659	136	49.0	.312	1.4	LF(150): -0.8	4.9
2020	WAS	MLB	21	630	133	43.6	.310	-0.1	LF 3	4.8

Position Players

After all that information and a thoughtful bylined essay covering each team, we present our player comments. These are also bylined, but due to frequent franchise shifts during the offseason, our bylines are more a rough guide than a perfect accounting of who wrote what.

Each player is listed with the major-league team that employed him as of early January 2020. If a player changed teams after that point via free agency, trade, or any other method, you'll be able to find them in the chapter for their previous squad.

As an example, take a look at the player comment for Nationals outfielder Juan Soto: the stat block that accompanies his written comment is at the top of this page. First we cover biographical information (age is as of June 30, 2020) before moving onto the stats themselves. Our statistic columns include standard identifying information like **YEAR**, **TEAM**, **LVL** (level of affiliated play) and **AGE** before getting into the numbers. Next, we provide raw, untranslated numbers like you might find on the back of your dad's baseball cards: **PA** (plate appearances), **R** (runs), **2B** (doubles), **3B** (triples), **HR** (home runs), **RBI** (runs batted in), **BB** (walks), **K** (strikeouts), **SB** (stolen bases) and **CS** (caught stealing).

Next, we have unadjusted "slash" statistics: **AVG** (batting average), **OBP** (on-base percentage) and **SLG** (slugging percentage). Following the slash line is **DRC+** (Deserved Runs Created Plus), which we described earlier as total offensive expected contribution compared to the league average.

One of our oldest active metrics, **VORP** (Value Over Replacement Player), considers offensive production, position and plate appearances. In essence, it is the number of runs contributed beyond what a replacement-level player at the same position would contribute if given the same percentage of team plate appearances. VORP does not consider the quality of a player's defense.

BABIP (batting average on balls in play) tells us how often a ball in play fell for a hit, and can help us identify whether a batter may have been lucky or not...but note that high BABIPs also tend to follow the great hitters of our time, as well as speedy singles hitters who put the ball on the ground.

The next item is **BRR** (Baserunning Runs), which covers all of a player's baserunning accomplishments including (but not limited to) swiped bags and failed attempts. Next is **FRAA** (Fielding Runs Above Average), which also includes the number of games previously played at each position noted in parentheses. Multi-position players have only their two most frequent positions listed here, but their total FRAA number reflects all positions played.

Our last column here is **WARP** (Wins Above Replacement Player). WARP estimates the total value of a player, which means for hitters it takes into account hitting runs above average (calculated using the DRC+ model), BRR and FRAA. Then, it makes an adjustment for positions played and gives the player a credit for plate appearances based upon the difference between "replacement level"—which is derived from the quality of players added to a team's roster after the start of the season–and the league average.

The final line just below the stats box is **PECOTA** data, which is discussed further in a following section.

Catchers

Catchers are a special breed, and thus they have earned their own separate box which displays some of the defensive metrics that we've built just for them. As an example, let's check out J.T. Realmuto.

The **YEAR** and **TEAM** columns match what you'd find in the other stat box. **P. COUNT** indicates the number of pitches thrown while the catcher was behind the plate, including swinging strikes, fouls and balls in play. **FRM RUNS** is the total run value the catcher provided (or cost) his team by influencing the umpire to call strikes where other catchers did not. **BLK RUNS** expresses the total run value above or below average for the catcher's ability to prevent wild pitches and passed balls. **THRW RUNS** is calculated using a similar model as the previous two statistics, and it measures a catcher's ability to throw out basestealers but also to dissuade them from testing his arm in the first place. It takes into account factors like the pitcher (including his delivery and pickoff move) and baserunner (who could be as fast as Billy Hamilton or as slow as Yonder Alonso). **TOT RUNS** is the sum of all of the previous three statistics.

Justin Verlander   RHP
Born: 02/20/83   Age: 37   Bats: R   Throws: R
Height: 6'5"   Weight: 225   Origin: Round 1, 2004 Draft (#2 overall)

YEAR	TEAM	LVL	AGE	W	L	SV	G	GS	IP	H	HR	BB/9	K/9	K	GB%	BABIP
2017	DET	MLB	34	10	8	0	28	28	172	153	23	3.5	9.2	176	34%	.283
2017	HOU	MLB	34	5	0	0	5	5	34	17	4	1.3	11.4	43	32%	.194
2018	HOU	MLB	35	16	9	0	34	34	214	156	28	1.6	12.2	290	31%	.272
2019	HOU	MLB	36	21	6	0	34	34	223	137	36	1.7	12.1	300	36%	.219
2020	HOU	MLB	37	15	6	0	29	29	184	138	28	2.3	12.1	248	35%	.274

Comparables: Zack Greinke, A.J. Burnett, Aníbal Sánchez

YEAR	TEAM	LVL	AGE	WHIP	ERA	DRA	WARP	MPH	FB%	WHF	CSP
2017	DET	MLB	34	1.28	3.82	4.03	3.0	97.7	58	11	47.8
2017	HOU	MLB	34	0.65	1.06	3.08	0.9	97.5	59.6	15.1	49.9
2018	HOU	MLB	35	0.90	2.52	2.33	7.3	97.5	61.2	16.2	51.6
2019	HOU	MLB	36	0.80	2.58	2.51	7.9	96.8	49.9	17.5	48.3
2020	HOU	MLB	37	1.01	2.75	2.95	5.3	95.8	54.6	15.1	48.2

Pitchers

Let's give our pitchers a turn, using 2019 AL Cy Young winner Justin Verlander as our example. Take a look at his stat block: the first line and the **YEAR**, **TEAM**, **LVL** and **AGE** columns are the same as in the position player example earlier.

Here too, we have a series of columns that display raw, unadjusted statistics compiled by the pitcher over the course of a season: **W** (wins), **L** (losses), **SV** (saves), **G** (games pitched), **GS** (games started), **IP** (innings pitched), **H** (hits allowed) and **HR** (home runs allowed). Next we have two statistics that are rates: **BB/9** (walks per nine innings) and **K/9** (strikeouts per nine innings), before returning to the unadjusted K (strikeouts).

Next up is **GB%** (ground ball percentage), which is the percentage of all batted balls that were hit on the ground, including both outs and hits. Remember, this is based on observational data and subject to human error, so please approach this with a healthy dose of skepticism.

BABIP (batting average on balls in play) is calculated using the same methodology as it is for position players, but it often tells us more about a pitcher than it does a hitter. With pitchers, a high BABIP is often due to poor defense or bad luck, and can often be an indicator of potential rebound, and a low BABIP may be cause to expect performance regression. (A typical league-average BABIP is close to .290-.300.)

The metrics **WHIP** (walks plus hits per inning pitched) and **ERA** (earned run average) are old standbys: WHIP measures walks and hits allowed on a per-inning basis, while ERA measures earned runs on a nine-inning basis. Neither of these stats are translated or adjusted.

DRA (Deserved Run Average) was described at length earlier, and measures how many runs the pitcher "deserved" to allow per nine innings. Please note that since we lack all the data points that would make for a "real" DRA for minor-league events, the DRA displayed for minor league partial-seasons is based off of different data. (That data is a modified version of our cFIP metric, which you can find more information about on our website.)

Just like with hitters, **WARP** (Wins Above Replacement Player) is a total value metric that puts pitchers of all stripes on the same scale as position players. We use DRA as the primary input for our calculation of WARP. You might notice that relief pitchers (due to their limited innings) may have a lower WARP than you were expecting or than you might see in other WARP-like metrics. WARP does not take leverage into account, just the actions a pitcher performs and the expected value of those actions...which ends up judging high-leverage relief pitchers differently than you might imagine given their prestige and market value.

MPH gives you the pitcher's 95th percentile velocity for the noted season, in order to give you an idea of what the *peak* fastball velocity a pitcher possesses. Since this comes from our pitch-tracking data, it is not publicly available for minor-league pitchers.

Finally, we display the three new pitching metrics we described earlier. **FB%** (fastball percentage) gives you the percentage of fastballs thrown out of all pitches. **WHF** (whiff rate) tells you the percentage of swinging strikes induced out of all pitches. **CSP** (called strike probability) expresses the likelihood of all pitches thrown to result in a called strike, after controlling for factors like handedness, umpire, pitch type, count and location.

PECOTA

All players have PECOTA projections for 2020, as well as a set of other numbers that describe the performance of comparable players according to PECOTA. All projections for 2020 are for the player at the date we went to press in early January and are projected into the league and park context as indicated by the team abbreviation. (Note that players at very low levels of the minors are too unpredictable to assess using these numbers.) All PECOTA projected statistics represent a player's projected major-league performance.

Below the projections are the player's three highest-scoring comparable players as determined by PECOTA. All comparables represent a snapshot of how the listed player was performing at the same age as the current player, so if a

23-year-old pitcher is compared to Bartolo Colón, he's actually being compared to a 23-year-old Colón, not the version that pitched for the Rangers in 2018, nor to Colón's career as a whole.

A few points about pitcher projections. First, we aren't yet projecting peak velocity, so that column will be blank in the PECOTA lines. Second, projecting DRA is trickier than evaluating past performance, because it is unclear how deserving each pitcher will be of his anticipated outcomes. However, we know that another DRA-related statistic–contextual FIP or cFIP-estimates future run scoring very well. So for PECOTA, the projected DRA figures you see are based on the past cFIPs generated by the pitcher and comparable players over time, along with the other factors described above.

Lineouts

In each chapter's Lineouts section, you'll find abbreviated text comments, as well as all the same information you'd find in our full player comments. The only difference is that we limit the stats boxes in this section to only including the 2019 information for each player.

Managers

After all those wonderful team chapters, we've got statistics for each big-league manager, all of whom are organized by alphabetical order. Here you'll find a block including an extraordinary amount of information collected from each manager's entire career. For more information on the acronyms and what they mean, please visit the Glossary at www.baseballprospectus.com.

There is one important metric that we'd like to call attention to, and you'll find it next to each manager's name: **wRM+** (weighted reliever management plus). Developed by Rob Arthur and Rian Watt, wRM+ investigates how good a manager is at using their best relievers during the moments of highest leverage, using both our proprietary DRA metric as well as Leverage Index. wRM+ is scaled to a league average of 100, and a wRM+ of 105 indicates that relievers were used approximately five percent "better" than average. On the other hand, a wRM+ of 95 would tell us the team used its relievers five percent "worse" than the average team.

While wRM+ does not have an extremely strong correlation with a manager, it is statistically significant; this means that a manager is not *entirely* responsible for a team's wRM+, but does have some effect on that number.

PECOTA Leaderboards

If you're familiar with PECOTA, then you'll have noticed that the projection system often appears bullish on players coming off a bad year and bearish on players coming off a good year. (This is because the system weights several previous seasons, not just the most recent one.) In addition, we publish the 50th

San Diego Padres 2020

percentile projections for each player—which is smack in the middle of the range of projected production—which tends to mean PECOTA stat lines don't often have extreme results like 40 home runs or 250 strikeouts in a given season. In essence, PECOTA doesn't project very many extreme seasons.

At the end of the book, we've ranked the top players at each position based on their PECOTA projections. This might help you visualize just how a given player's projection compares to that of their peers, so that even if a dramatic stat line isn't projected, you can still imagine how they stack up against the rest of the league.

Part 1: Team Analysis

San Diego Padres: Where Are You Going, Where Have You Been?

Jarrett Seidler, Wilson Karaman and Matthew Trueblood

2019: What Went Right
The high point for the 2019 Padres come on February 19th. That was the day they agreed to terms with star infielder Manny Machado on a 10-year deal. He represented a rarity, a superstar player with a very broad base of skills hitting free agency at just 26. General manager A.J. Preller swooped in on the eve of the season and plucked him away from the White Sox and others. Machado provides a cornerstone that the Padres will be able to build around well into the 2020s.

The other franchise cornerstone emerged just a few months later. Fernando Tatís Jr. entered 2019 as one of the three best prospects in the world, but with only just a little over a half-season in the high-minors on his baseball card. He won the shortstop job out of camp, and for the 84 games he played was one of the absolute best players in the game. He displayed every ability you can display on the diamond, hitting .317 with walks and power while displaying flashy shortstop defense and incredible athleticism. Tatís missed six weeks early in the season with a hamstring injury, and a back injury ended his season early. Yet nothing can take away from his pure dominance at just 20 years old. He'll lock down the left side of the infield along with Machado for many years to come.

Tatís wasn't the only top Padres prospect who emerged in March. Chris Paddack made the jump to the big-league rotation out of camp too. He quickly validated lofty projections by befuddling hitters with his dazzling fastball/changeup combination. Though he looked more vulnerable as the season progressed, he remains one of baseball's most promising young pitchers.

Franmil Reyes hit balls very hard and sometimes very far for the Padres from April through July. The burly slugger mashed 27 taters in just 99 games, which is impressive even in the age of the juiced ball. Preller took that as a sign to cash out at the deadline, pairing Reyes with pitching prospect Logan Allen and complex flier Victor Nova to get involved in the Trevor Bauer trade between Cleveland

and Cincinnati. The Padres got back outfielder Taylor Trammell in the exchange. After a disappointing season, Trammell fell down the prospect-rankings boards, but he retains a high upside. We still rank him fifth among the Padres top 10 prospects, but he needs to develop his power tool to be an impact player. That said, considering that Reyes wasn't a perfect fit for a National League squad and Allen was already being overtaken by better pitching prospects, acquiring a potential star in Trammell was a nice bit of risk/reward gambling.

2019: What Went Wrong

San Diego was a trendy pick to contend for the wild card last year. You don't spend $300 million on one of baseball's best players if you're not trying to win. While San Diego surpassed 2018's win total, they remained mired in the slough of mediocrity that has held the franchise in its grip since 2011. Is there still value in a slow journey to the top? Only with the benefit of hindsight after one has arrived. The Padres are a lot closer to figuring out who will be on the next good Padres team over the past year, and that's something. They've uncovered some surprises along the way like Reyes and closer Kirby Yates and started to figure out which young guys are the true keepers.

Not all of those are answers they'll like, of course. Austin Hedges and Manuel Margot are settling in as defensive specialists who may never hit. Francisco Mejía is by no means a lost cause, but he hasn't been the immediate success that prospects with similar potential have been. The starting pitching behind Paddack hasn't really sorted itself out yet, although the two best talents in MacKenzie Gore and Luis Patiño are yet to come. At least Méjia is still here; Luis Urías was dealt to the Brewers in November in return for veteran starter Zach Davies and 2019 rookie outfielder Trent Grisham.

The big free agent moves haven't been all roses yet, either. Machado had a down year at the plate by his standards. If you're worried about a long-term problem, he hit especially poorly at Petco (.219/.297/.406 versus .289/.369/.513 on the road). He shouldn't be much of a concern moving forward, but that's a large contract to live up to, and neither the park nor the marine layer are going anywhere.

Eric Hosmer's deal—eight years at $144 million—was a reach the second it was signed. At his best, as in 2017 for the Royals, Hosmer is roughly a .300 hitter who provides enough in defense and gap power to be worth that sort of salary. He's had four of those seasons in a nine-year career, none as yet for the Padres. At .259/.316/.412 in Padres' blue, he's provided below-average offensive production that his defense simply can't carry. He's graded out as exactly a replacement player for his first 300 games. The 2020 campaign will be his age-30 season, a red flag even if he were still producing at peak levels. The Padres are committed to him for another six years. He's going to need to turn it around in a big way, because right now it's hard to even say that he's a much better first base option than Josh Naylor moving forward. —*Jarret Seidler*

Prospect Outlook

The reigning best system in baseball has graduated four of its top five prospects this year, and yet the system remains well-entrenched among the elite ranks of the sport. Two first-round shortstops have jumped to the top rungs of the system and been joined by a third, yet another teenaged arm has exploded up everyone's pref lists, and the mid-season addition of **Taylor Trammell** has rounded the top of the system out in Saturday night style once again.

In a more ordinary system, we might begin with a couple of high-ceilinged, big-league 2019 toe-dippers like pitchers **Adrian Morejon** and **Michel Baez**, both of whom have flashed legitimate middle-of-the-rotation potential. Trammell intrigues with the spark his athleticism could bring to the top of an emerging lineup. And in a normal system, either of those options would be just-fine things to hang your hat on.

This isn't a normal system, though, and neither is the kid who leads it. There will be a workload to manage after he threw 101 innings this year between the High- and Double-A levels, but barring injury **MacKenzie Gore** should make his anticipated debut in America's Finest City sometime next season. How rapidly he establishes himself will go a long way in determining just when/if the Friars can emerge as a competitive counterweight to LA's divisional dominance. His is a special profile, and if Gore plays to full potential as quickly as soon-to-be rotation-mate Paddack did, a camouflaged challenge from the south could very well arrive on the doorstep of the Azul sooner than anticipated. —*Wilson Karaman*

2020 Outlook

In the final analysis, San Diego's season was frustrating. As many bright spots as there were, the team made no tangible wins-and-losses progress toward unseating the Dodgers in 2019. As a result, Preller decided that it was time for another of his signature shakeups. Out went Andy Green and in came Jayce Tingler, a longtime Rangers front office staffer and coach with whom Preller was familiar from his time in player development in Texas. The sparkling farm system Preller has cultivated over the last few years can best pay dividends if the team's major league philosophy and practice with regard to that development is coherent. Tingler's arrival nudges them in that direction.

However, there were also glaring holes on the roster—deficiencies not easily papered over by better instruction or development. Preller took a similarly aggressive tack with those. A three-trade shuffle sent Urías, Renfroe, and a handful of young players out the door, and brought in Jurickson Profar (with whom both Preller and Tingler have a certain measure of comfortable history), Tommy Pham, and Trent Grisham. The net effect was to tilt the team's balance between youth and experience, between risk and safety, between athleticism and on-base percentage a bit toward the latter. With more top prospects on the way, that was a wise choice.

What Preller did not do this time around was make a big splash in free agency. Speculation that he might try to bring Stephen Strasburg back to the town where he played college ball went for naught. San Diego re-signed Craig Stammen, went to a fourth year to nab Drew Pomeranz, and solidified one of the deepest bullpens in baseball. They also made a small but potentially significant upgrade by getting Davies in the Urías-Grisham trade. If the back end of the rotation and the bottom half of the lineup hold up while the best of the reinforcements marinate just a bit more, this team is dangerous, and for the first time in three years, Preller has kept a little powder dry. —*Matthew Trueblood*

Performance Graphs

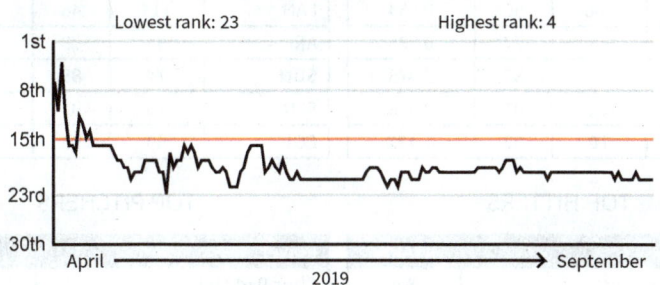

2019 Hit List Ranking

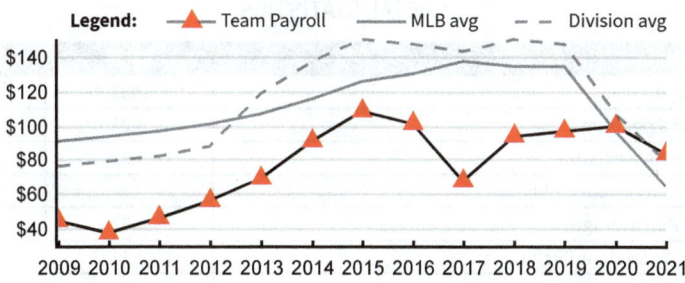

Committed Payroll (in millions)

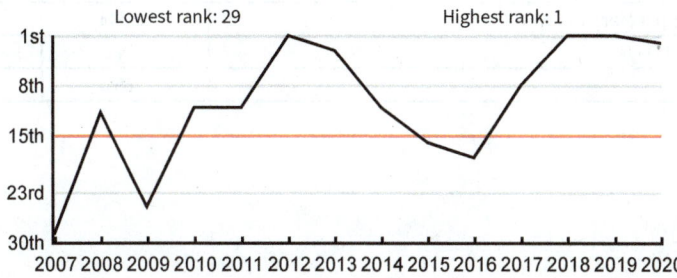

Farm System Ranking

2019 Team Performance

ACTUAL STANDINGS

Team	W	L	Pct
LAN	106	56	0.654
ARI	85	77	0.525
SFN	77	85	0.475
COL	71	91	0.438
SDN	**70**	**92**	**0.432**

THIRD-ORDER STANDINGS

Team	W	L	Pct
LAN	114	48	0.702
ARI	84	78	0.516
SDN	**74**	**88**	**0.454**
SFN	70	92	0.431
COL	69	93	0.429

TOP HITTERS

Player	WARP
Fernando Tatis Jr.	3.4
Austin Hedges	2.9
Franmil Reyes	1.6

TOP PITCHERS

Player	WARP
Chris Paddack	4.0
Joey Lucchesi	2.9
Kirby Yates	2.2

VITAL STATISTICS

Statistic Name	Value	Rank
Pythagenpat	.432	22nd
Runs Scored per Game	4.21	27th
Runs Allowed per Game	4.87	17th
Deserved Runs Created Plus	84	27th
Deserved Run Average	4.33	9th
Fielding Independent Pitching	4.17	8th
Defensive Efficiency Rating	.701	18th
Batter Age	26.0	2nd
Pitcher Age	25.9	1st
Salary	$97.2M	23rd
Marginal $ per Marginal Win	$3.9M	15th
Injured List Days	1971	28th
$ on IL	15%	16th

2020 Team Projections

PROJECTED STANDINGS

Team	W	L	Pct	+/-
LAN	102.5	59.5	0.633	-4
SDN	**79.3**	**82.7**	**0.490**	**9**
ARI	78.9	83.1	0.487	-6
COL	76.6	85.4	0.473	6
SFN	68.4	93.6	0.422	-9

TOP PROJECTED HITTERS

Player	WARP
Fernando Tatis Jr.	3.5
Manny Machado	2.0
Tommy Pham	1.9

TOP PROJECTED PITCHERS

Player	WARP
Chris Paddack	3.2
Garrett Richards	2.2
Dinelson Lamet	1.9

FARM SYSTEM REPORT

Top Prospect	Number of Top 101 Prospects
MacKenzie Gore, #5	7

KEY DEDUCTIONS

Player	WARP
Luis Urías	1.8
Hunter Renfroe	1.6
Eric Lauer	0.9
Austin Allen	0.8
Carl Edwards Jr.	0.8
Manuel Margot	0.2
Travis Jankowski	0.1
Nick Martini	0.1
Robbie Erlin	0.1
Robert Stock	0.0

KEY ADDITIONS

Player	WARP
Tommy Pham	1.9
Emilio Pagán	1.2
Trent Grisham	1.0
Zach Davies	0.7
Brian Dozier	0.4
MacKenzie Gore	0.4
Drew Pomeranz	0.3
Esteban Quiroz	0.2
Jurickson Profar	0.2
Pierce Johnson	0.2

Team Personnel

Executive Vice President, General Manager
A.J. Preller

Vice President, Assistant General Manager
Fred Uhlman, Jr.

Senior Advisor/Director of Player Personnel
Logan White

Assistant General Manager
Josh Stein

Manager
Jayce Tingler

BP Alumni
David Cameron

Petco Park Stats

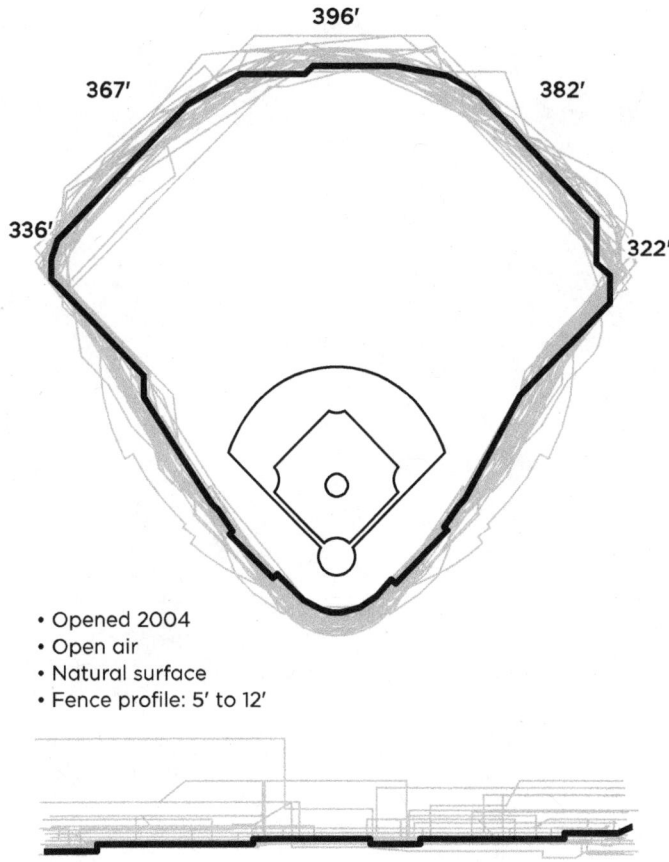

- Opened 2004
- Open air
- Natural surface
- Fence profile: 5' to 12'

Three-Year Park Factors

Runs	Runs/RH	Runs/LH	HR/RH	HR/LH
96	97	94	96	91

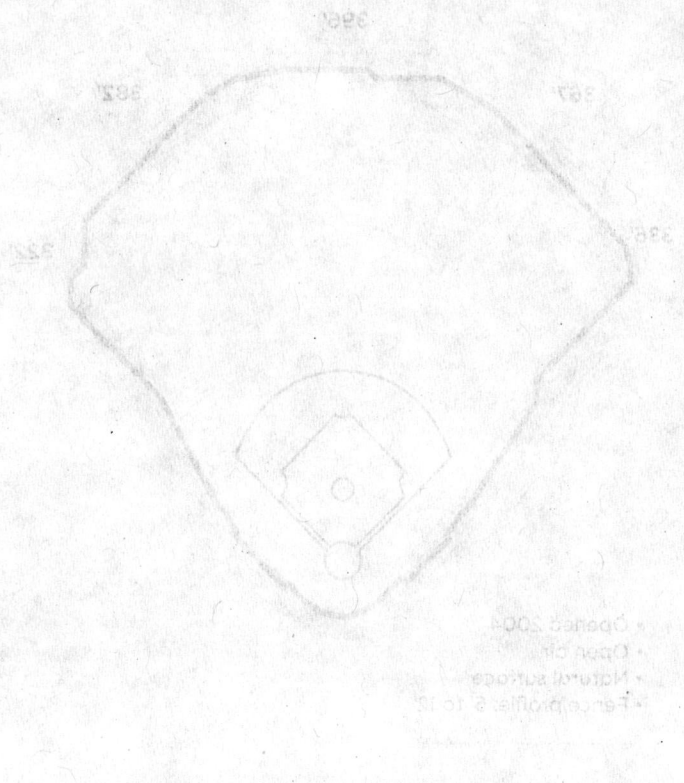

Padres Team Analysis

What does a color mean? For a sports team, mostly it's marketing; a way to sell merchandise. But if you step away from the cynicism for a moment, can it be more than that? Can a team's colors be representative of its soul?

In early November, the San Diego Padres held a ceremony at Petco Park to unveil a change that fans had wanted for more than a decade and the team finally agreed to and announced prior to the 2019 season: After nearly 20 years of dabbling in all kinds of blue-hued uniform color combinations—remember Ryan Klesko and Sean Burroughs running around the bases in cobalt and "sand" in the early aughts?—the team was finally going back to wearing brown.

For most baseball fans outside of San Diego, the hoopla surrounding the unveiling must have seemed ridiculous. Everyone could agree that the new uniforms looked good—the home ones, with brown pinstripes contrasted against a white background and gold trim, especially—but what was the big deal?

Why would thousands of fans head to Petco for a fashion show? Remember, this is a franchise that has ranked 10th or worse in attendance in the National League in 11 of the past 12 seasons. It takes a lot to get Padres fans to show up.

But in reality, it was about more than a uniform color. The Padres, a franchise that once proudly wore mustard and brown, had finally found their true selves again.

"This is going to be the uniform we select and win a championship in," Ron Fowler, the executive chairman of the Padres, said in a video that was shown before Fernando Tatis Jr., Manny Machado and Eric Hosmer walked onstage in the new uniforms. The new/old team colors were so well received that Padres fans couldn't even be bothered to boo Hosmer.

The ceremony felt like the start of something new—even though none of us Padres fans really know what that means—it just feels different. For the first time that I can remember, there are high expectations and a genuine enthusiasm, a sense that we're about to witness something special.

For one night, even the wonderful and wacked out collection of people who make up #PadresTwitter—I would argue as antagonistic a group of baseball fans that you'll find on social media—could agree on one thing: This was a good night! (This doesn't happen very often on #PadresTwitter. More often it's one part of #PadresTwitter ridiculing the other part because they think Luis Urías will eventually hit .280. He's #BrewersTwitter's problem now.)

Even if it doesn't turn out that San Diego is on the verge of success, just the sheer audacity of Fowler, and fans, to think in these ways—championships, MVPs and dynasties—belies an atmosphere that has never existed. The days of the passive Padres fan are over. Welcome to the win-at-all-costs era. We think this team should win, and if it doesn't, then we have all concluded that everyone in the front office should be fired.

Each Padres follower has a unique path into this particular fandom. It's hard to say that anyone in San Diego naturally becomes attached to the franchise. Who would choose to suffer through so many losing seasons?

But geography does play a part in why it's such a unique fanbase. Firstly, San Diego has always been known as a city of transplants. An analysis of 2017 census data published recently by the *Voice of San Diego* showed that more than half of all San Diegans were born outside of California. Also, only a third of those between the ages of 35 and 44 were born in state, they noted.

Such factors have helped to create a fractured fan base. For most of my time growing up in San Diego, and for the last several years, it was not uncommon for Padres games to be inundated with fans from the opposing team; it was natural since so many people in the city were from somewhere else. This was especially true of games against the Dodgers. Embarrassingly, Los Angeles fans almost always outnumber Padres fans at Petco.

But San Diego's demographics are changing at the same time the Padres' uniforms are changing. The article noted that the crash of the housing market has caused fewer people to move to San Diego. The percentage of San Diegans from San Diego is increasing. More people are considering themselves to be from San Diego than from elsewhere. They have a bigger attachment to the city.

And these demographic changes come at an opportune time. The Chargers moved to Los Angeles several years ago, leaving San Diego as a one-team town. But of course that one team has to be good in order to truly win over fans.

⚾ ⚾ ⚾

I became a Padres fan mostly because of proximity. I was born across the border in Tijuana, Mexico, and my family moved to San Diego when I was five years old. I grew up in San Ysidro, just a few miles away from the border crossing. I became a San Diegan.

And I loved baseball. But mostly, I loved the Padres. My parents have told me that I could recite the entire Padres lineup by the time I was four years old. (I'm not sure what it says about my parents that they were so proud that I could say "Terry Kennedy" at such a young age).

But even fandom-by-proximity can be tested. Around that time, Fernando Valenzuela was becoming an icon for the Dodgers. His immediate success coupled with his Mexican heritage made it natural for him to become my family's favorite player, and perhaps the Dodgers would become my family's new favorite team. It seemed like every other Mexican we knew was a Dodgers fan.

And it seemed we were headed that way too—before an unfortunate encounter changed everything.

This particular story has been told many times by different members of my family, each version slightly different than the previous, but it boils down to this: When I was very young, so young that I hardly remember any of this, my cousin and I staked out the players' exit after a Dodgers vs. Padres game at Jack Murphy Stadium (the former home of the Padres that was gloriously for many years named after a sportswriter and then was not so gloriously named for the telecommunications company Qualcomm and now is just named SDCCU Stadium because no one wants to pay money for the sponsorship rights), waiting for autographs.

In one version, we waited nearly an hour after the game. In other versions, it's much longer than that. None of the players were coming out, but we were not going to be denied. Eventually, several players emerged and signed our cards, but our real target was Fernando. So we continued to wait. And wait. And then we waited some more. Finally, Fernando emerged to a crowd that had been thinned by the long wait.

We shouted for Fernando to stop, pleading with him in English and Spanish, but he walked right past us. We didn't exist to him. He just walked away. That simple act of non-acknowledgement sealed the deal. After that, my family's fandom was unequivocally decided: We were Padres fans, and we hated the Dodgers.

It would be easy to say that this decision has turned out badly for us. But I wouldn't have wanted it to happen any other way.

Not too many years after the incident with Fernando, my father scored tickets to Game 4 of the 1984 National League Championship Series. We sat in the upper deck as Steve Garvey hit a walk-off home run against Lee Smith of the Chicago Cubs. I remember high fiving every person near us. Everyone seemed amused at my excitement. The Padres would eventually win that best-of-five series after having lost the first two games.

Unfortunately, the Detroit Tigers trounced them in the World Series. I wept for days afterward. Such is life as a Padres fan; some rare moments of excitement and a lot of crying.

There was perhaps more crying during the early-90s run of Tom Werner's ownership than any other. Werner oversaw trades that ended the tenures of players like Gary Sheffield and Fred McGriff, and despite a mere four-year term as majority owner, Werner nearly sunk the franchise with his actions. And that's not even accounting for his decision to introduce blue and orange into the Padres' color scheme in 1991; a decision the team didn't reverse until this coming season.

The most emblematic image of the Padres to that point, was of Tony Gwynn, already in his 10th season but still in the prime of his career, balanced as ever, stroking base hits through the 5.5 hole draped in a monk-ish brown. That he notched hit number 3,000 in a sparsely populated Olympic Stadium was unfortunate; that it happened in the drab, disaffecting grays and blues? Despicable.

I was lucky enough that in a previous life as a sportswriter—I'm currently an editor in news at *The New York Times*—that I was able to interview Gwynn after he had retired. We talked for about an hour in the Petco Park dugout. Of course, we talked hitting. But I also told him about how I used to attend his hitting camps when I was a kid, wearing that brown Padres hat. I told him how much his career had meant to me, and how much I loved his Padres teams as a kid. He seemed genuinely touched even though he'd probably had this similar conversation thousands of times.

Surprisingly, Werner's color legacy remained untouched for years after his disastrous era of ownership ended. The team's primary color stayed blue. In a sense, it seemed as though fans would never escape the Werner era.

But now here we are; the colors are brown again, and the team has the potential to really be exciting. In the last few years, they've spent significant money bringing in high-profile free agents, which is something they had never done. The farm system is stacked. This is the complete opposite of the Werner era.

And we're excited about it, even if we all show our excitement in different ways. Almost certainly, #PadresTwitter will debate the prognostications for Padres players that will follow this essay in the book, and bless them all. These are my people.

Many will argue that the Padres need to trade some of their young talent for established players. Others will call those people irrational and passionately argue the opposite. (For what it's worth, my thoughts after the 2019 season are to hold onto MacKenzie Gore, and to consider trading Luis Patiño in the right deal.) But at least we have something interesting to argue about. It seems so long ago that we wondered about whether Alexi Amarista was the second baseman of the future.

So when someone asks whether a uniform color really means anything, the answer is yes. Sure, the Padres are going to sell a lot of jerseys and hats because they're back in brown. And that was certainly part of the motivation. But we're all going to feel a lot better about spending some of our money on that merchandise. It won't feel like we've given away our soul to wear blue.

—Jorge Arangure Jr. is a senior editor at The New York Times.

Part 2: Player Analysis

PLAYER COMMENTS WITH GRAPHS

Ty France 3B
Born: 07/13/94 Age: 25 Bats: R Throws: R
Height: 6'0" Weight: 205 Origin: Round 34, 2015 Draft (#1017 overall)

YEAR	TEAM	LVL	AGE	PA	R	2B	3B	HR	RBI	BB	K	SB	CS	AVG/OBP/SLG
2017	LEL	A+	22	131	10	4	2	0	19	7	16	1	0	.288/.389/.360
2017	SAN	AA	22	402	42	20	1	5	39	22	68	1	0	.275/.341/.377
2018	SAN	AA	23	479	66	22	2	17	77	33	70	3	4	.263/.349/.448
2018	ELP	AAA	23	110	18	8	0	5	19	13	19	0	0	.287/.382/.532
2019	ELP	AAA	24	348	83	27	1	27	89	30	51	1	0	.399/.477/.770
2019	SDN	MLB	24	201	20	8	1	7	24	9	49	0	2	.234/.294/.402
2020	SDN	MLB	25	112	14	5	0	5	15	7	26	0	0	.250/.325/.449

Comparables: Evan Longoria, Ed Sprague, Earl Robinson

France's El Paso numbers border on the ridiculous and are reminiscent of a total solar eclipse: they're stunningly beautiful, and if you stare at them too long their white-hot glare will burn your retinas, but don't hold your breath expecting to see them again any time soon. The former 34th-round pick laid waste to the juiced-ball PCL and earned two big-league call-ups where his solid power showed up but his contact skills and admirable walk rate disappeared. France is a good hitter, not a great one, especially in the context of major-league corner men. He's a second baseman in the same way Matt Carpenter is a second baseman, more out of necessity and willingness than a true talent for the position, which means he'll have a higher offensive bar to clear at third or first base. Truly elite batting talent will always make itself known, but at this point France looks more like a solid bench piece than a star in waiting.

YEAR	TEAM	LVL	AGE	PA	DRC+	VORP	BABIP	BRR	FRAA	WARP
2017	LEL	A+	22	131	113	3.8	.333	-0.9	1B(13): -0.2, 3B(4): 0.0	0.2
2017	SAN	AA	22	402	103	15.4	.325	0.5	3B(85): -8.8, 1B(7): 0.2	0.5
2018	SAN	AA	23	479	124	23.8	.276	1.3	3B(101): -7.7, 1B(1): 0.0	2.0
2018	ELP	AAA	23	110	130	7.8	.310	0.6	3B(19): 2.8, 1B(9): 0.1	1.1
2019	ELP	AAA	24	348	183	49.6	.410	1.0	3B(31): -1.8, 1B(29): -2.3	3.7
2019	SDN	MLB	24	201	77	1.4	.279	0.4	3B(36): -0.6, 2B(21): 2.2	0.3
2020	SDN	MLB	25	112	106	5.1	.289	0.3	2B 0, 3B 0	0.5

Ty France, continued

Batted Ball Distribution

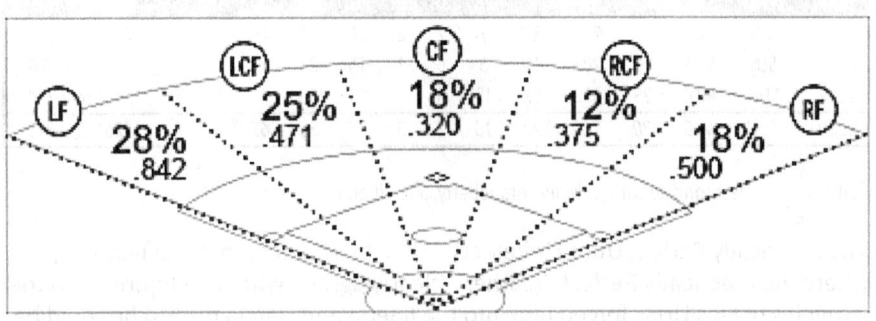

Strike Zone vs LHP   **Strike Zone vs RHP**

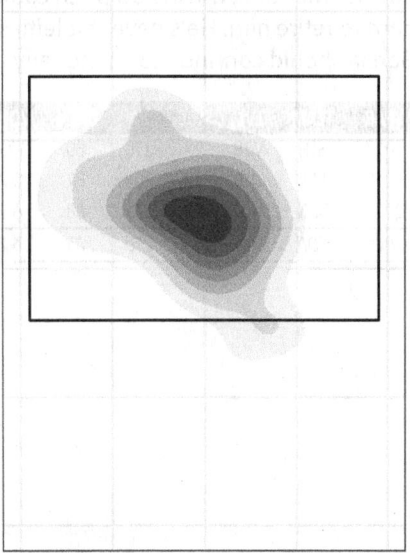

Greg Garcia   INF

Born: 08/08/89   Age: 30   Bats: L   Throws: R
Height: 6'0"   Weight: 190   Origin: Round 7, 2010 Draft (#229 overall)

YEAR	TEAM	LVL	AGE	PA	R	2B	3B	HR	RBI	BB	K	SB	CS	AVG/OBP/SLG
2017	SLN	MLB	27	290	27	9	2	2	20	37	64	2	1	.253/.365/.332
2018	SLN	MLB	28	208	15	6	0	3	15	20	37	3	1	.221/.309/.304
2019	SDN	MLB	29	372	52	13	4	4	31	53	83	0	2	.248/.364/.354
2020	SDN	MLB	30	280	27	10	1	3	23	35	62	4	1	.226/.335/.313

Comparables: Desmond Jennings, Marv Throneberry, Joe Vitiello

The Practically Perfect Utility Infielder™ moved home to San Diego last year, where the Practically Perfect Weather™ clearly agreed with him. Injuries and the struggles of Luis Urías forced him into the lineup and Garcia proved he could be a passable platoon starter at the keystone when his usual menu of walks, singles and steady defense proved as tasty in the first inning as the seventh. Garcia sorts through pitches like a chef at a farmer's market, rarely offering at anything outside the zone, driving up pitch counts and making opposing hurlers work hard to retire him. He's never hit lefties and is a little stretched at shortstop, but Garcia should continue to bolster any team that employs him well into his 30s.

YEAR	TEAM	LVL	AGE	PA	DRC+	VORP	BABIP	BRR	FRAA	WARP
2017	SLN	MLB	27	290	80	13.4	.335	3.8	3B(41): 1.1, 2B(34): 0.5	0.8
2018	SLN	MLB	28	208	81	0.2	.259	0.2	2B(31): -0.4, SS(17): 1.9	0.4
2019	SDN	MLB	29	372	88	6.9	.323	2.4	2B(74): 2.1, 3B(13): -0.6	1.1
2020	SDN	MLB	30	280	83	6.2	.292	1.6	2B -1, SS 0	0.6

Greg Garcia, continued

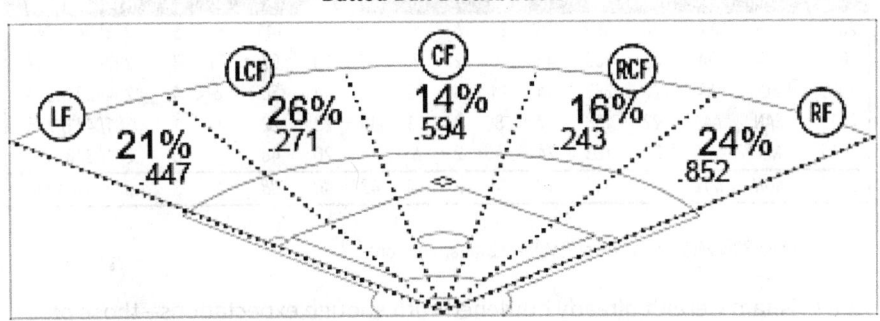

Batted Ball Distribution

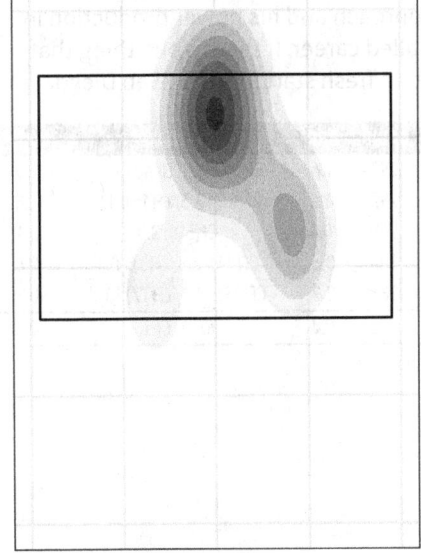

Strike Zone vs LHP

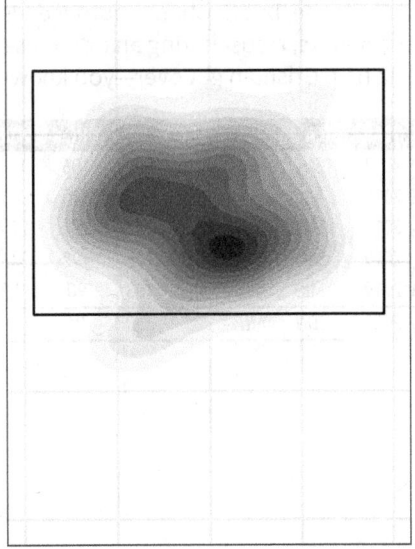

Strike Zone vs RHP

Trent Grisham OF

Born: 11/01/96 Age: 23 Bats: L Throws: L
Height: 6'0" Weight: 205 Origin: Round 1, 2015 Draft (#15 overall)

YEAR	TEAM	LVL	AGE	PA	R	2B	3B	HR	RBI	BB	K	SB	CS	AVG/OBP/SLG
2017	CAR	A+	20	569	78	21	6	8	45	98	141	37	5	.223/.360/.348
2018	BLX	AA	21	405	45	10	2	7	31	63	87	11	3	.233/.356/.337
2019	BLX	AA	22	283	34	14	3	13	41	44	50	6	4	.254/.371/.504
2019	SAN	AAA	22	158	37	8	3	13	30	23	22	6	1	.381/.471/.776
2019	MIL	MLB	22	183	24	6	2	6	24	20	48	1	0	.231/.328/.410
2020	SDN	MLB	23	350	40	14	2	12	42	40	88	9	3	.224/.318/.404

Comparables: Billy McKinney, Victor Robles, Abraham Almonte

As if Grisham weren't already burdened with enough expectations—those of being a former top prospect and first-round pick—his misplay in the Wild Card Game added another layer to the onion. That reality is unfortunate for a number of reasons, in part because it obscured how hard he'd worked in order to reach the point of starting in a postseason game. Sure, Christian Yelich's injury was the main cause, but Grisham improved his approach and his power production in the minors, resuscitating an otherwise stalled career. If there's one thing that will help Grisham get over—you know—it's a fresh start in sunny San Diego.

YEAR	TEAM	LVL	AGE	PA	DRC+	VORP	BABIP	BRR	FRAA	WARP
2017	CAR	A+	20	569	106	14.2	.299	1.6	RF(52): 1.5, LF(40): -0.5	1.9
2018	BLX	AA	21	405	110	7.1	.292	-1.8	RF(85): 3.5, LF(15): 1.1	1.8
2019	BLX	AA	22	283	162	22.4	.269	-0.4	CF(59): 3.3	3.1
2019	SAN	AAA	22	158	192	31.4	.384	0.3	CF(31): 3.3, LF(3): -0.1	2.6
2019	MIL	MLB	22	183	90	3.2	.286	2.2	CF(21): -1.1, LF(17): -1.8	0.3
2020	SDN	MLB	23	350	96	7.9	.273	0.4	RF -1, CF 0	0.7

Trent Grisham, continued

Batted Ball Distribution

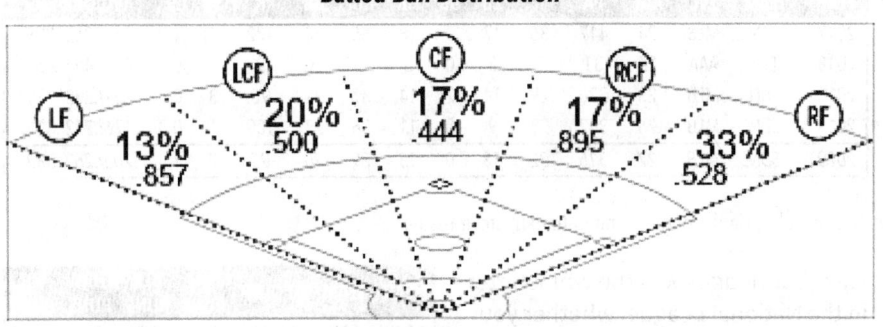

Strike Zone vs LHP

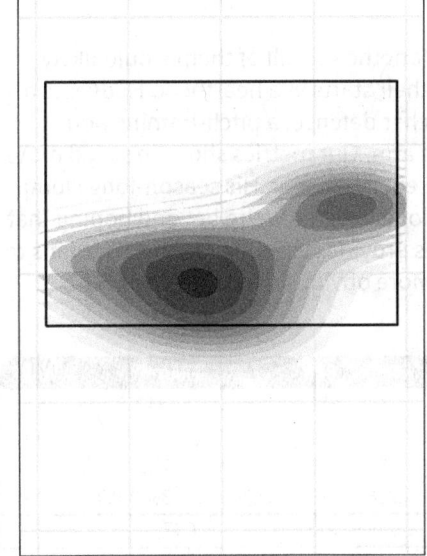

Strike Zone vs RHP

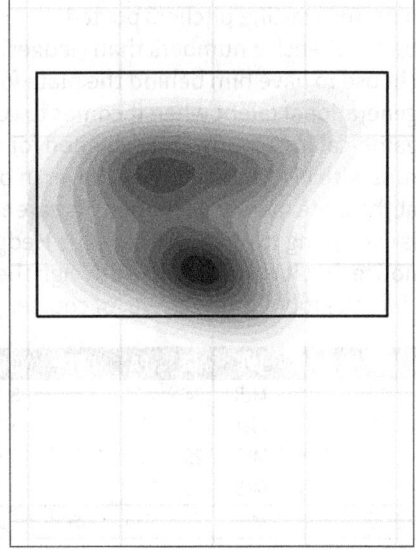

San Diego Padres 2020

Austin Hedges C

Born: 08/18/92   Age: 27   Bats: R   Throws: R
Height: 6'1"   Weight: 206   Origin: Round 2, 2011 Draft (#82 overall)

YEAR	TEAM	LVL	AGE	PA	R	2B	3B	HR	RBI	BB	K	SB	CS	AVG/OBP/SLG
2017	SDN	MLB	24	417	36	17	0	18	55	23	122	4	1	.214/.262/.398
2018	ELP	AAA	25	31	7	3	0	3	11	3	9	0	0	.407/.452/.852
2018	SDN	MLB	25	326	29	14	2	14	37	21	90	3	0	.231/.282/.429
2019	SDN	MLB	26	347	28	9	0	11	36	27	109	1	0	.176/.252/.311
2020	SDN	MLB	27	315	32	12	0	13	39	20	93	2	1	.206/.262/.383

Comparables: Hank Conger, John Bateman, Steve Yeager

YEAR	TEAM	P. COUNT	FRM RUNS	BLK RUNS	THRW RUNS	TOT RUNS
2017	SDN	15353	28.0	1.3	2.2	30.3
2018	SDN	11915	13.0	0.1	-0.4	12.6
2019	SDN	13445	26.0	1.5	0.3	27.8
2020	SDN	12242	14.6	1.2	0.7	16.5

Last year Hedges was the worst hitter in the National League, whether you want to determine such a thing using classic rock (Batting Average), punk/new wave (OPS) or hip hop (DRC+) measures. Jarrod Dyson out-slugged him. Ten starting pitchers posted better offensive numbers than Hedges. Nonetheless, all of them would likely choose to have him behind the plate for their starts in a heartbeat. Hedges is a generational talent when it comes to catcher defense, a pitch-framing and game-calling savant with a cannon for an arm. Our metrics show he saved more runs with his glove than any player in baseball last year. His season-long slump at the plate merely deepened his career-long rut, and we're beyond hoping that is ever going to change. The value Hedges provides is subtle and hard for fans to notice, but it continues to outweigh the more obvious dead weight of his bat. Until the robot umps arrive, of course.

YEAR	TEAM	LVL	AGE	PA	DRC+	VORP	BABIP	BRR	FRAA	WARP
2017	SDN	MLB	24	417	75	8.3	.260	0.6	C(115): 34.1	4.2
2018	ELP	AAA	25	31	151	6.2	.500	0.0	C(6): 0.5	0.4
2018	SDN	MLB	25	326	88	8.1	.280	-2.1	C(83): 11.8	2.1
2019	SDN	MLB	26	347	61	0.7	.228	0.9	C(95): 28.2, 3B(2): 0.0	2.9
2020	SDN	MLB	27	315	69	1.6	.254	-0.3	C 17	1.9

Austin Hedges, continued

Batted Ball Distribution

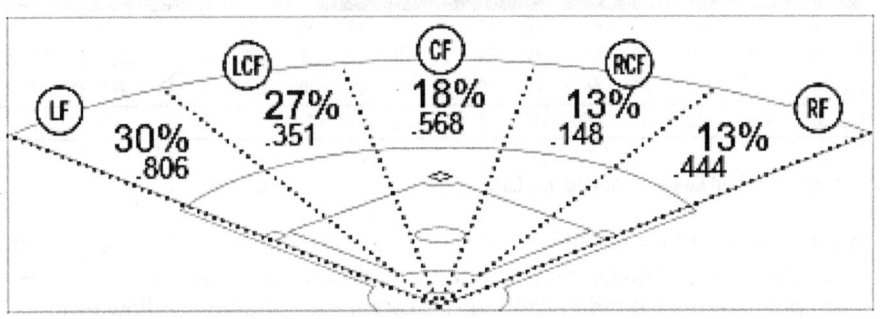

Strike Zone vs LHP   Strike Zone vs RHP

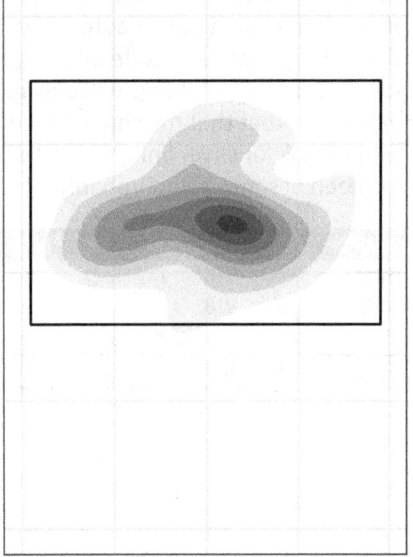

San Diego Padres 2020

Eric Hosmer 1B

Born: 10/24/89   Age: 30   Bats: L   Throws: L
Height: 6'4"   Weight: 225   Origin: Round 1, 2008 Draft (#3 overall)

YEAR	TEAM	LVL	AGE	PA	R	2B	3B	HR	RBI	BB	K	SB	CS	AVG/OBP/SLG
2017	KCA	MLB	27	671	98	31	1	25	94	66	104	6	1	.318/.385/.498
2018	SDN	MLB	28	677	72	31	2	18	69	62	142	7	4	.253/.322/.398
2019	SDN	MLB	29	667	72	29	2	22	99	40	163	0	3	.265/.310/.425
2020	SDN	MLB	30	630	67	26	2	20	74	48	145	5	2	.254/.313/.407

Comparables: Paul Konerko, Torii Hunter, Casey Kotchman

If you're looking for a bright side in the $92 million Hosmer is still owed, well, at least his contract is no longer the largest in Padres history. If you were disappointed Hosmer didn't continue his career-long pattern of following up bad seasons with relatively good ones, well, maybe the pattern is just switching to two-off, one-on. If you thought Hosmer was still a Gold Glove-caliber first baseman, well, short-term defensive slumps are actually a thing. If you're disappointed that we don't have flying cars yet, well, at least we're on the verge of autonomous electric scooters. If you're horrified by Hosmer's woeful numbers against same-side pitching, well, at least lefties are in the minority. If you're worried that things will only get worse as Hosmer moves into his thirties, well, remember that the shape of the aging curve is a guideline, not a rule. If you tend to look for silver linings in even the darkest of clouds, well, we hope this has been of some help. Probably it hasn't.

YEAR	TEAM	LVL	AGE	PA	DRC+	VORP	BABIP	BRR	FRAA	WARP
2017	KCA	MLB	27	671	126	35.9	.351	-1.3	1B(157): 0.6	3.0
2018	SDN	MLB	28	677	84	-1.2	.302	-2.6	1B(157): 7.8	0.1
2019	SDN	MLB	29	667	86	-1.9	.323	-0.2	1B(157): -3.9	-0.6
2020	SDN	MLB	30	630	94	6.1	.307	-1.0	1B 0	0.6

Eric Hosmer, continued

Batted Ball Distribution

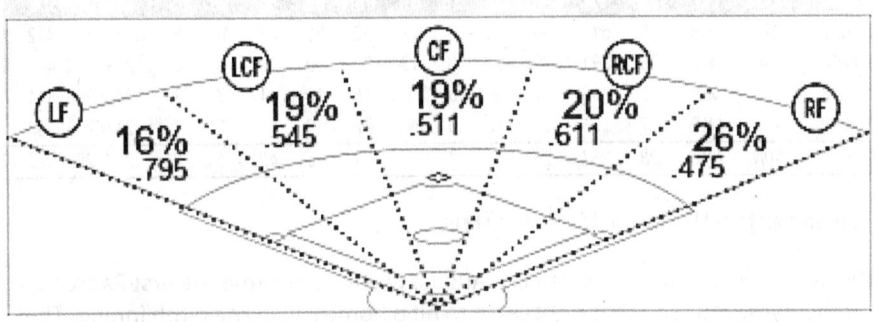

Strike Zone vs LHP   **Strike Zone vs RHP**

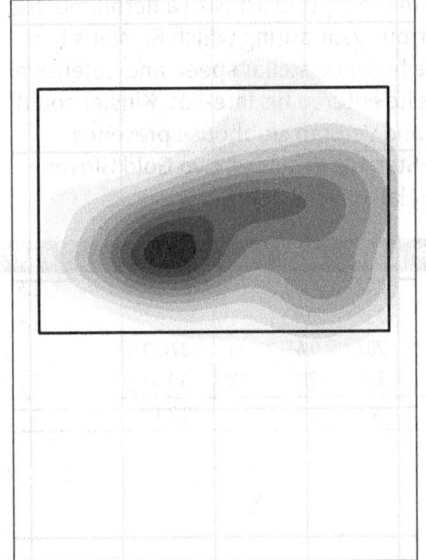 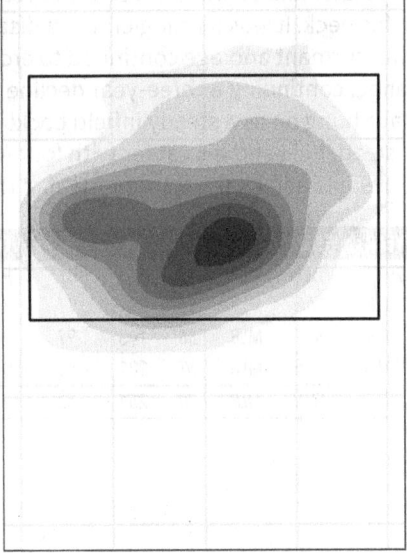

San Diego Padres 2020

Ian Kinsler 2B

Born: 06/22/82   Age: 38   Bats: R   Throws: R
Height: 6'0"   Weight: 200   Origin: Round 17, 2003 Draft (#496 overall)

YEAR	TEAM	LVL	AGE	PA	R	2B	3B	HR	RBI	BB	K	SB	CS	AVG/OBP/SLG
2017	DET	MLB	35	613	90	25	3	22	52	55	86	14	5	.236/.313/.412
2018	LAA	MLB	36	391	49	20	0	13	32	30	40	9	4	.239/.304/.406
2018	BOS	MLB	36	143	17	6	0	1	16	10	24	7	3	.242/.294/.311
2019	SDN	MLB	37	281	28	12	0	9	22	19	54	2	4	.217/.278/.368
2020	SDN	MLB	38	251	26	11	1	8	29	16	47	5	2	.234/.290/.392

Comparables: Mark Ellis, Asdrúbal Cabrera, Jeff Kent

Kinsler made San Diego history last August when he became the first Padres pitcher (yes, you read that right) ever to hit a home run in the ninth inning. The veteran second-sacker took the mound in garbage time and allowed four baserunners but no runs before launching a meaningless two-run bomb in the bottom half. It was his last game of the season, as Kinsler awoke in pain two days later and spent the rest of the year on the injured list with a herniated disc in his neck. It was a fitting end to a disastrous year during which Kinsler's bat was dormant and age continued to erode his once-stellar speed and defensive range, continuing a three-year decline as he entered his late-30s. Kinsler could have hung on as a steady infield backup and veteran clubhouse presence. Instead, he'll end his career with four All-Star appearances, two Gold Gloves, 1,999 hits and likely enshrinement in the Hall of Very Good.

YEAR	TEAM	LVL	AGE	PA	DRC+	VORP	BABIP	BRR	FRAA	WARP
2017	DET	MLB	35	613	102	9.5	.244	4.7	2B(135): 1.0	2.6
2018	LAA	MLB	36	391	97	7.8	.237	-0.9		1.4
2018	BOS	MLB	36	143	97	-3.1	.287	0.6	2B(37): -1.3	0.3
2019	SDN	MLB	37	281	75	0.5	.240	-2.7	2B(72): 3.1, P(1): 0.0	0.1
2020	SDN	MLB	38	251	82	2.5	.261	0.3	2B 1	0.4

Ian Kinsler, continued

Batted Ball Distribution

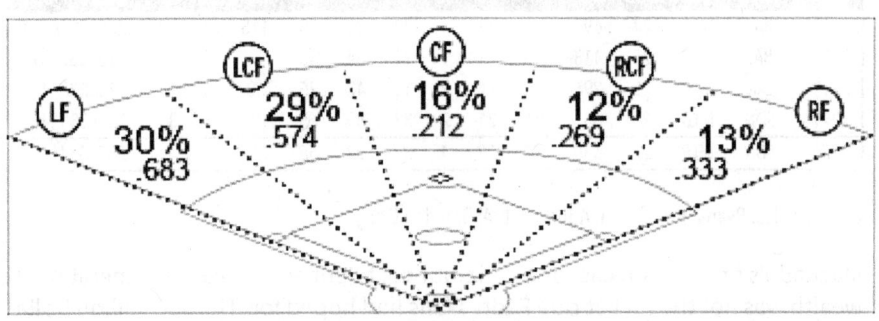

Strike Zone vs LHP   **Strike Zone vs RHP**

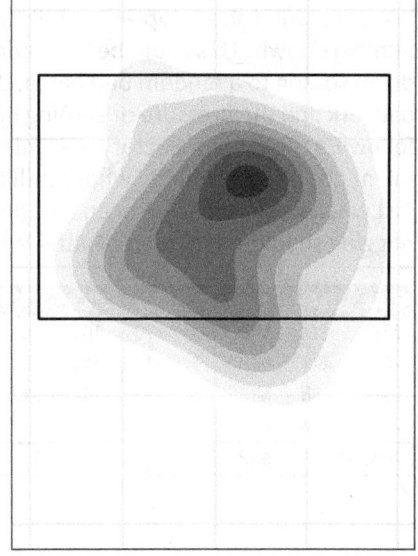

San Diego Padres 2020

Manny Machado 3B
Born: 07/06/92 Age: 27 Bats: R Throws: R
Height: 6'3" Weight: 215 Origin: Round 1, 2010 Draft (#3 overall)

YEAR	TEAM	LVL	AGE	PA	R	2B	3B	HR	RBI	BB	K	SB	CS	AVG/OBP/SLG
2017	BAL	MLB	24	690	81	33	1	33	95	50	115	9	4	.259/.310/.471
2018	BAL	MLB	25	413	48	21	1	24	65	45	51	8	1	.315/.387/.575
2018	LAN	MLB	25	296	36	14	2	13	42	25	53	6	1	.273/.338/.487
2019	SDN	MLB	26	661	81	21	2	32	85	65	128	5	3	.256/.334/.462
2020	SDN	MLB	27	630	81	29	1	31	92	58	119	9	4	.262/.334/.479

Comparables: Ryan Zimmerman, Adrián Beltré, Brandon Drury

Machado's first season cast as a generational talent accumulating generational wealth was not the rocket ride Padres fans had hoped for. The 300 Million Dollar Man was not an elite offensive force, as he was frequently bedeviled by breaking stuff and off-speed junk and posted disturbing platoon (.239/.315/.400 against righties) and home/road (.219/.297/.406 at Petco) splits. Machado's leatherwork at the hot corner was plus but not spectacular, and the month he spent Jetering his way around shortstop—hopefully for the last time—dragged his overall numbers down. This could be Machado's floor going forward, chalking up a down season to a random bad patch, difficulty adjusting to a run-suppressing ballpark and the pressure of earning his massive salary. Or … he could be following the same trajectory as Hanley Ramírez, another prodigious infield talent accused of lethargy whose brilliant early career similarly began its decline just when he should have been entering his peak (aided, admittedly, by a nagging shoulder injury). A healthy Machado should be able to avoid that fate.

YEAR	TEAM	LVL	AGE	PA	DRC+	VORP	BABIP	BRR	FRAA	WARP
2017	BAL	MLB	24	690	106	20.8	.265	-4.1	3B(156): -6.2	2.0
2018	BAL	MLB	25	413	141	40.3	.311	-0.5	SS(96): -4.5	3.5
2018	LAN	MLB	25	296	142	21.5	.296	1.4	SS(51): -4.5, 3B(16): 3.1	2.8
2019	SDN	MLB	26	661	106	32.4	.274	-1.3	3B(119): -10.4, SS(37): -5.2	1.5
2020	SDN	MLB	27	630	114	25.7	.282	-1.7	3B -5, SS -1	2.0

Manny Machado, continued

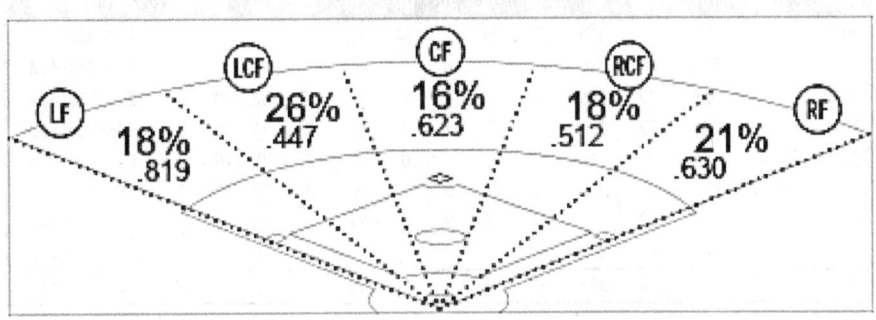

Strike Zone vs LHP   **Strike Zone vs RHP**

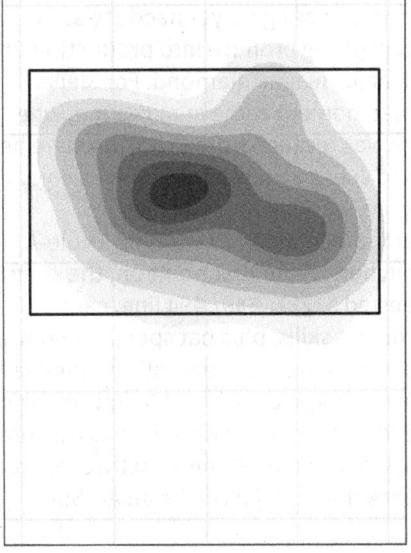

San Diego Padres 2020

Francisco Mejía C

Born: 10/27/95   Age: 24   Bats: B   Throws: R
Height: 5'10"   Weight: 180   Origin: International Free Agent, 2012

YEAR	TEAM	LVL	AGE	PA	R	2B	3B	HR	RBI	BB	K	SB	CS	AVG/OBP/SLG
2017	AKR	AA	21	383	52	21	2	14	52	24	53	7	2	.297/.346/.490
2017	CLE	MLB	21	14	1	0	0	0	1	1	3	0	0	.154/.214/.154
2018	COH	AAA	22	336	32	22	1	7	45	18	58	0	0	.279/.328/.426
2018	ELP	AAA	22	132	22	8	1	7	23	7	25	0	0	.328/.364/.582
2018	CLE	MLB	22	4	0	0	0	0	0	2	0	0	0	.000/.500/.000
2018	SDN	MLB	22	58	6	2	0	3	8	3	19	0	0	.185/.241/.389
2019	ELP	AAA	23	73	14	8	2	4	12	5	10	0	0	.365/.411/.746
2019	SDN	MLB	23	244	27	11	2	8	22	13	56	1	1	.265/.316/.438
2020	SDN	MLB	24	364	39	16	1	14	46	20	82	1	0	.241/.293/.417

Comparables: John Ryan Murphy, Ronald Guzmán, Dominic Smith

YEAR	TEAM	P. COUNT	FRM RUNS	BLK RUNS	THRW RUNS	TOT RUNS
2017	AKR	9761	-0.5	-0.8	-0.1	0.7
2017	CLE	40	0.0	0.0	0.0	3.2
2018	COH	5559	2.6	0.7	0.3	3.8
2018	ELP	3547	0.0	0.0	0.2	0.6
2018	SDN	1484	-0.7	-0.8	0.0	-0.7
2019	ELP	2085	1.9	0.0	0.0	1.9
2019	SDN	7679	-0.8	0.1	-0.5	-1.3
2020	SDN	12848	-1.3	-1.1	-1.0	-3.4

Mejía has been one of baseball's top prospects for years now, but at some point, a young player needs to start converting promise into production on a major-league diamond. For Mejía, that moment came in mid-June, when he was recalled from El Paso, where he had spent a month rehabbing a sore knee, working on defensive fundamentals and tattooing Triple-A pitchers. From that point on, the switch-hitting catcher with the rocket arm posted a .297/.349/.494 line, earning more and more playing time. His advanced contact skills, plus bat speed and power potential left few doubting the backstop would eventually hit big-league pitching. Just as importantly, Mejía seems more committed to improving on his poor play behind the dish, and the Padres seem convinced he has the tools to stay there. He graded out near average in our catching metrics last year, and if he can at least not be a liability back there, Mejía will be an All-Star.

YEAR	TEAM	LVL	AGE	PA	DRC+	VORP	BABIP	BRR	FRAA	WARP
2017	AKR	AA	21	383	133	32.6	.311	1.5	C(72): 1.6, 3B(1): -0.1	3.3
2017	CLE	MLB	21	14	78	-1.7	.200	-0.3	C(3): 0.0	0.0
2018	COH	AAA	22	336	102	9.4	.321	-1.2	C(41): 4.6, LF(22): -3.2	1.2
2018	ELP	AAA	22	132	121	11.8	.359	0.7	C(26): 1.3	1.1
2018	CLE	MLB	22	4	69	0.1	.000	0.0		0.0
2018	SDN	MLB	22	58	73	-0.3	.219	0.2	C(10): -1.7	-0.1
2019	ELP	AAA	23	73	136	9.3	.365	-1.0	C(16): 2.6	0.8
2019	SDN	MLB	23	244	90	9.0	.319	2.0	C(60): -0.6, LF(4): 0.3	1.0
2020	SDN	MLB	24	364	91	13.9	.278	1.3	C -2	1.3

San Diego Padres 2020

Francisco Mejía, continued

Batted Ball Distribution

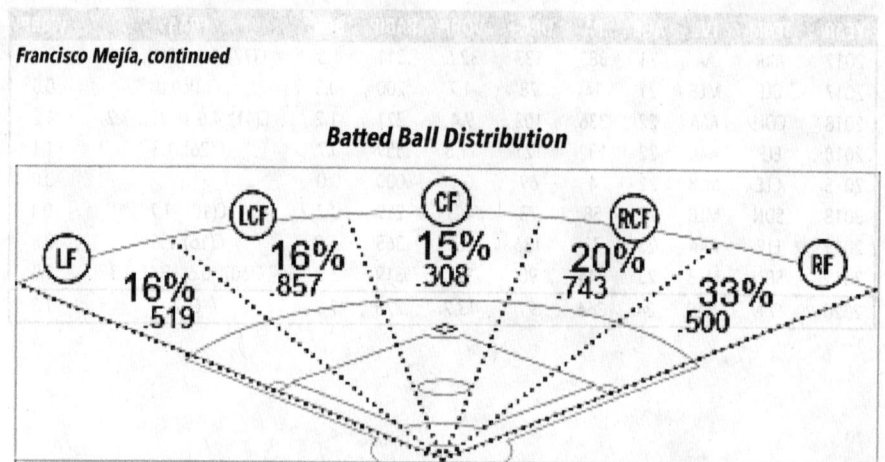

Strike Zone vs LHP **Strike Zone vs RHP**

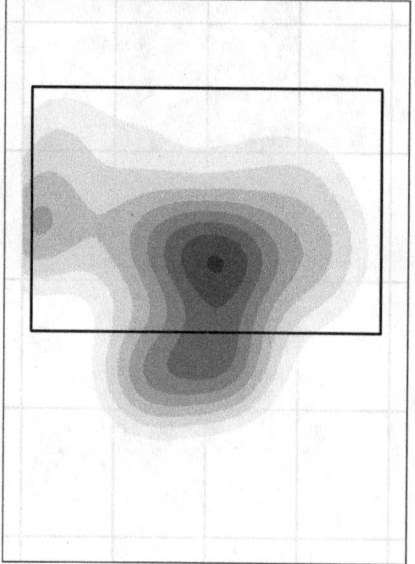

Wil Myers OF

Born: 12/10/90 Age: 29 Bats: R Throws: R
Height: 6'3" Weight: 205 Origin: Round 3, 2009 Draft (#91 overall)

YEAR	TEAM	LVL	AGE	PA	R	2B	3B	HR	RBI	BB	K	SB	CS	AVG/OBP/SLG
2017	SDN	MLB	26	649	80	29	3	30	74	70	180	20	6	.243/.328/.464
2018	SDN	MLB	27	343	39	25	1	11	39	30	94	13	1	.253/.318/.446
2019	SDN	MLB	28	490	58	22	1	18	53	51	168	16	7	.239/.321/.418
2020	SDN	MLB	29	301	35	13	1	11	37	31	99	9	3	.230/.313/.413

Comparables: Jay Bruce, Justin Upton, Jesse Barfield

New position. New hair. New teammates. Same result. Myers showed up this year sporting tinted Baywatch locks and looking ready to make a new start in left field, but struggled through his most disappointing season yet. Pitchers fed him a steady diet of high fastballs and sliders away and Myers kept swinging through them, helping his strikeout rate soar to a National League worst 34.4 percent while his power continued to dwindle. The Padres, perhaps thinking it would be easier to lower the floor than raise the stairs, tried him in center field but his misadventures there leaked so much value he ended the year as essentially a replacement-level player. Nearing 30 and set to earn $68.5 million over the next three years, Myers is as obvious a change-of-scenery candidate as there is in baseball.

YEAR	TEAM	LVL	AGE	PA	DRC+	VORP	BABIP	BRR	FRAA	WARP
2017	SDN	MLB	26	649	108	28.2	.297	1.1	1B(154): -1.8	1.4
2018	SDN	MLB	27	343	91	14.7	.327	1.3	3B(36): -4.3, LF(31): 0.8	0.6
2019	SDN	MLB	28	490	85	5.6	.344	-1.6	LF(98): -2.8, CF(66): -1.1	0.0
2020	SDN	MLB	29	301	94	5.2	.318	-0.1	RF 4, CF 0	0.9

San Diego Padres 2020

Wil Myers, continued

Batted Ball Distribution

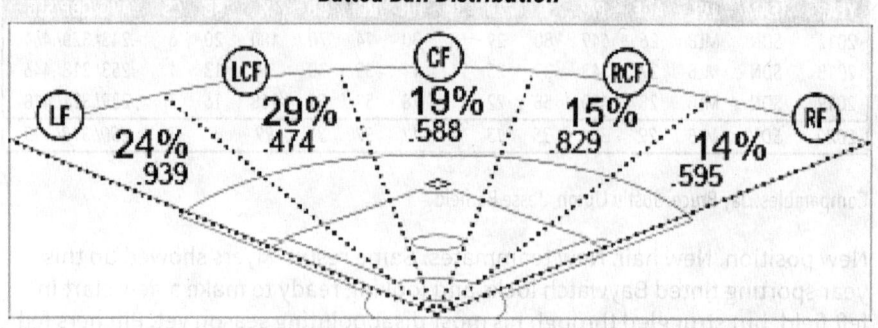

Strike Zone vs LHP

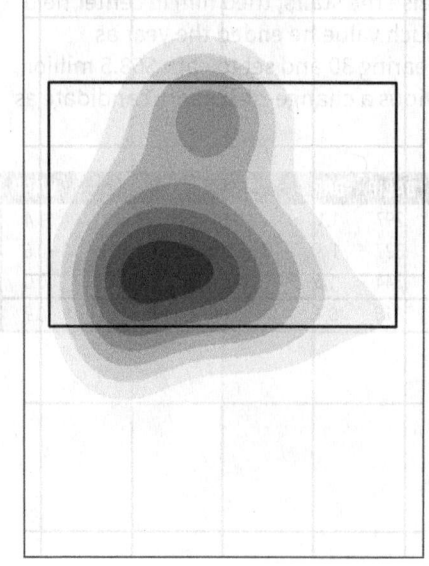

Strike Zone vs RHP

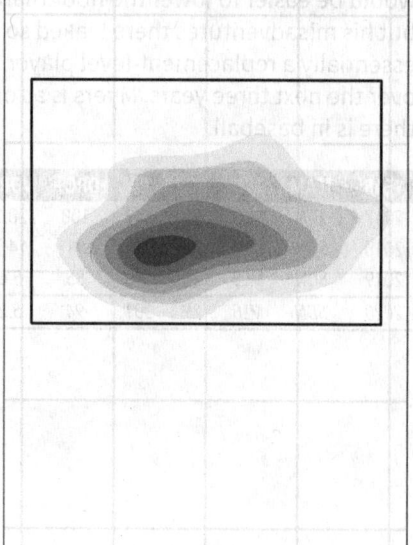

Josh Naylor RF

Born: 06/22/97 Age: 23 Bats: L Throws: L
Height: 5'11" Weight: 250 Origin: Round 1, 2015 Draft (#12 overall)

YEAR	TEAM	LVL	AGE	PA	R	2B	3B	HR	RBI	BB	K	SB	CS	AVG/OBP/SLG
2017	LEL	A+	20	313	41	16	2	8	45	27	48	7	1	.297/.361/.452
2017	SAN	AA	20	175	18	9	0	2	19	16	36	2	1	.250/.320/.346
2018	SAN	AA	21	574	72	22	1	17	74	64	69	5	5	.297/.383/.447
2019	ELP	AAA	22	252	51	20	1	10	42	28	30	1	0	.314/.389/.547
2019	SDN	MLB	22	279	29	15	0	8	32	25	64	1	1	.249/.315/.403
2020	SDN	MLB	23	273	28	14	1	7	30	22	56	1	1	.243/.308/.394

Comparables: Dominic Smith, Cole Tucker, Josh Vitters

Blocked at first base by Eric Hosmer's passbook, the Padres tried to get Naylor's estimable bat into the lineup some other way, with predictable results. The young Canuck is a Large Adult Son of the first order who should be taking pot shots at some AL stadium's short porch in right and spitting seeds between plate appearances, not shagging flies in Petco's vast expanses. Naylor has a preternatural feel for contact, an advanced approach and tremendous raw power that remains on back-order for game day but feels about ready to arrive.

YEAR	TEAM	LVL	AGE	PA	DRC+	VORP	BABIP	BRR	FRAA	WARP
2017	LEL	A+	20	313	135	14.5	.333	-0.1	1B(42): -0.6	1.4
2017	SAN	AA	20	175	100	1.1	.308	-0.9	1B(40): 1.9	0.3
2018	SAN	AA	21	574	142	27.3	.317	-5.1	LF(89): -20.4, 1B(29): 0.6	0.9
2019	ELP	AAA	22	252	118	11.9	.326	0.0	RF(29): -2.2, LF(22): 1.0	1.0
2019	SDN	MLB	22	279	82	0.5	.302	-0.2	LF(33): 0.7, RF(31): -4.1	-0.3
2020	SDN	MLB	23	273	90	3.2	.286	0.0	RF -6, LF -1	-0.3

San Diego Padres 2020

Josh Naylor, continued

Batted Ball Distribution

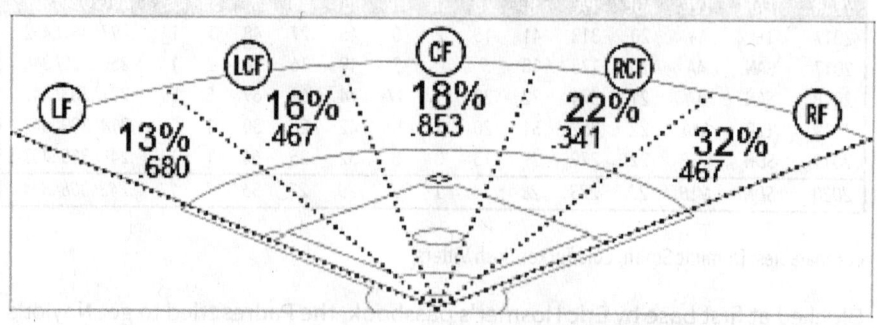

Strike Zone vs LHP

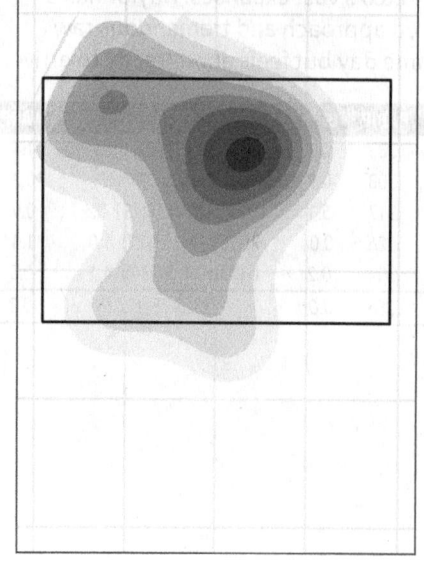

Strike Zone vs RHP

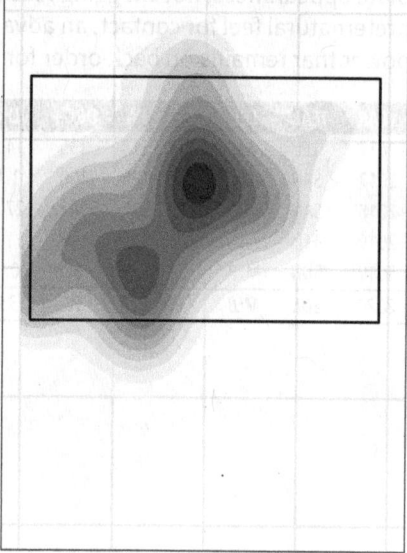

Tommy Pham LF
Born: 03/08/88 Age: 32 Bats: R Throws: R
Height: 6'1" Weight: 215 Origin: Round 16, 2006 Draft (#496 overall)

YEAR	TEAM	LVL	AGE	PA	R	2B	3B	HR	RBI	BB	K	SB	CS	AVG/OBP/SLG
2017	MEM	AAA	29	106	17	8	0	4	19	13	21	6	3	.283/.371/.500
2017	SLN	MLB	29	530	95	22	2	23	73	71	117	25	7	.306/.411/.520
2018	SLN	MLB	30	396	67	11	0	14	41	42	97	10	6	.248/.331/.399
2018	TBA	MLB	30	174	35	7	6	7	22	25	43	5	1	.343/.448/.622
2019	TBA	MLB	31	654	77	33	2	21	68	81	123	25	4	.273/.369/.450
2020	SDN	MLB	32	595	72	24	2	20	72	71	126	18	6	.254/.350/.424

Comparables: Matthew den Dekker, Brad Wilkerson, Marcus Thames

Pham was not as good as he was in the second half of 2018 for the Rays, but he was good nonetheless, and arguably the team's most consistent performer over the course of the year. At one point, he racked up a team-record, 48-game on-base streak that carried over from the 2018 season. For the second time over the last three campaigns, he reached the 20/20 plateau. In fact, he tallied the dubious distinction of going 20/20/20 if you add in the 22 times he grounded into double plays—the first player to do that since Ryan Braun in 2015. Defensively, he was limited to left field where he did not make an error. That said, it's hard to make errors on balls you don't get to. The outspoken outfielder took on more of a leadership role for the young Rays club and was often to the go-to guy for an opinion on things happening around the team. Of course, if they want that opinion in 2020, they'll have to dial long-distance as Pham was traded to San Diego just before the Winter Meetings.

YEAR	TEAM	LVL	AGE	PA	DRC+	VORP	BABIP	BRR	FRAA	WARP
2017	MEM	AAA	29	106	125	9.1	.328	0.7	RF(15): 2.2, CF(9): -1.0	0.8
2017	SLN	MLB	29	530	140	58.2	.368	4.6	LF(86): -2.6, CF(37): 0.1	4.3
2018	SLN	MLB	30	396	122	18.6	.303	3.8	CF(91): -5.1	2.3
2018	TBA	MLB	30	174	121	21.2	.442	0.9	LF(37): -0.5, CF(3): -0.2	0.9
2019	TBA	MLB	31	654	116	30.6	.316	-0.2	LF(123): -9.6	2.0
2020	SDN	MLB	32	595	109	24.8	.300	2.1	LF -8	1.7

San Diego Padres 2020

Tommy Pham, continued

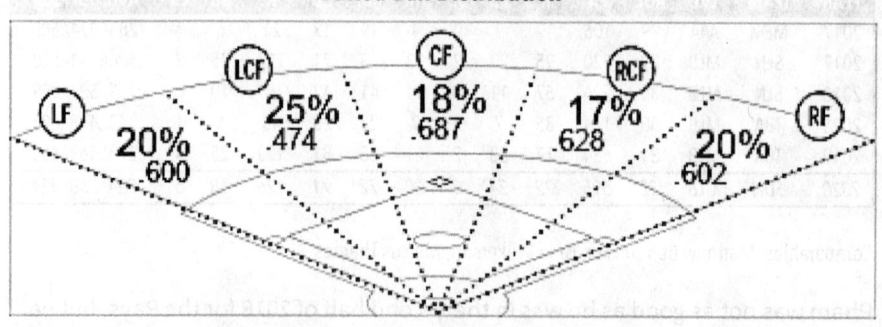

Batted Ball Distribution

- LF: 20% .600
- LCF: 25% .474
- CF: 18% .687
- RCF: 17% .628
- RF: 20% .602

Strike Zone vs LHP

Strike Zone vs RHP

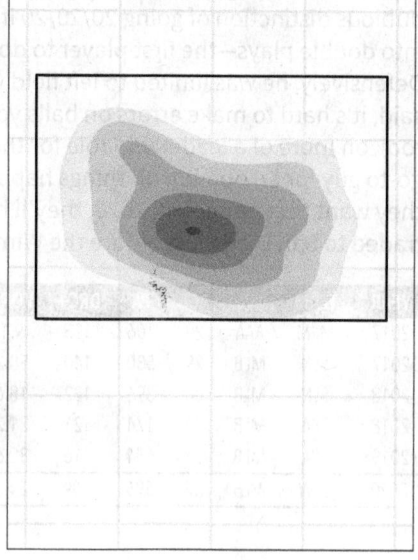

Jurickson Profar 2B

Born: 02/20/93 Age: 27 Bats: B Throws: R
Height: 6'0" Weight: 190 Origin: International Free Agent, 2009

YEAR	TEAM	LVL	AGE	PA	R	2B	3B	HR	RBI	BB	K	SB	CS	AVG/OBP/SLG
2017	ROU	AAA	24	383	50	25	0	7	45	43	33	5	0	.287/.383/.428
2017	TEX	MLB	24	70	8	2	0	0	5	9	14	1	1	.172/.294/.207
2018	TEX	MLB	25	594	82	35	6	20	77	54	88	10	0	.254/.335/.458
2019	OAK	MLB	26	518	65	24	2	20	67	48	75	9	1	.218/.301/.410
2020	SDN	MLB	27	497	53	23	2	16	57	46	77	5	2	.222/.306/.390

Comparables: Dustin Ackley, Gordon Beckham, Rougned Odor

The nasty part about the yips is that practice can't really cure the disease. Much like stage fright, you simply can't simulate the conditions that produce the problem; Steve Sax could throw the ball to first just fine in practice, it was the game state that changed everything. Following an offseason trade and a positional switch, the yips came for Profar, who made six throwing errors in the first month of the season. Between those and many other unnatural looking tosses, it became clear what he was up against. From there, Profar battled. His throws were not always pretty: His arm slot changed, his release point came and went, the ball sometimes bounced on its way in. Ultimately though, his throws managed to find their destination more often than not. Whatever his DRS and DRC, that's a triumph, and hopefully it's one that clears the runway for bigger and better things going forward in San Diego.

YEAR	TEAM	LVL	AGE	PA	DRC+	VORP	BABIP	BRR	FRAA	WARP
2017	ROU	AAA	24	383	117	33.2	.302	2.9	SS(78): -6.6, 2B(3): -0.2	2.2
2017	TEX	MLB	24	70	76	-0.8	.227	0.8	LF(12): 1.2, SS(4): -0.6	0.1
2018	TEX	MLB	25	594	110	28.6	.269	2.2	SS(68): -8.6, 3B(51): -3.7	1.8
2019	OAK	MLB	26	518	97	14.5	.218	0.4	2B(124): -12.5, LF(7): 0.0	0.2
2020	SDN	MLB	27	497	90	12.0	.236	0.5	2B -8, 3B 0	0.4

Jurickson Profar, continued

Batted Ball Distribution

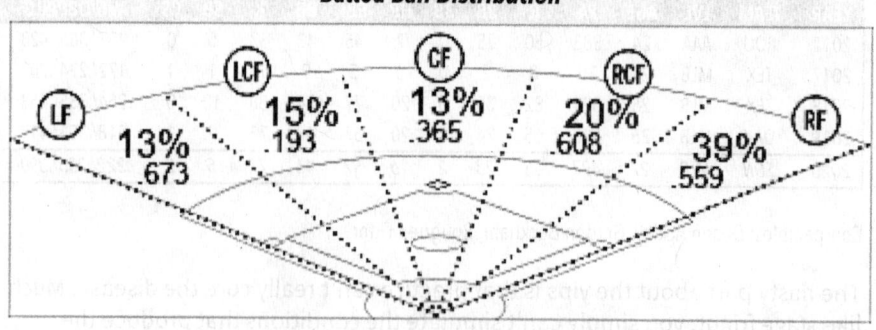

Strike Zone vs LHP

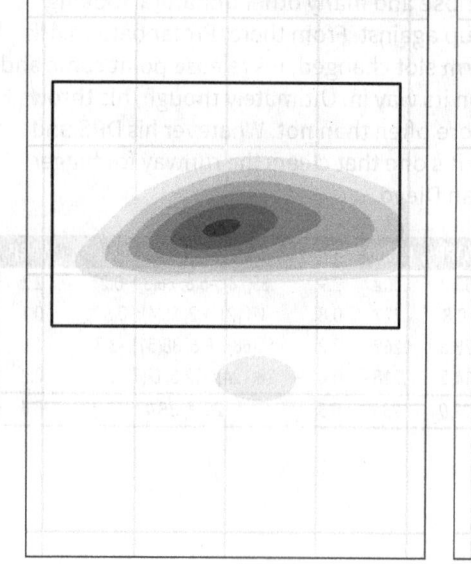

Strike Zone vs RHP

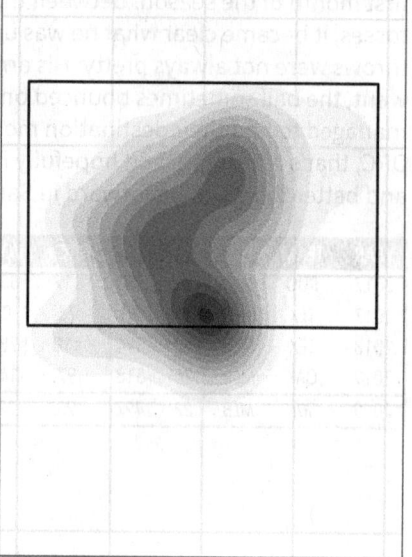

Fernando Tatís Jr. SS

Born: 01/02/99 Age: 21 Bats: R Throws: R
Height: 6'3" Weight: 185 Origin: International Free Agent, 2015

YEAR	TEAM	LVL	AGE	PA	R	2B	3B	HR	RBI	BB	K	SB	CS	AVG/OBP/SLG
2017	FTW	A	18	518	78	26	7	21	69	75	124	29	15	.281/.390/.520
2017	SAN	AA	18	57	6	1	0	1	6	2	17	3	0	.255/.281/.327
2018	SAN	AA	19	394	77	22	4	16	43	33	109	16	5	.286/.355/.507
2019	SDN	MLB	20	372	61	13	6	22	53	30	110	16	6	.317/.379/.590
2020	SDN	MLB	21	595	72	26	4	26	81	43	175	17	7	.256/.316/.458

Comparables: Carlos Correa, Rougned Odor, Ronald Acuña Jr.

You know it when you see it, and you definitely saw it. Over 84 games last year Tatís unleashed his abundant talent, athleticism and exuberance in ballparks nationwide, stealing bases, smothering ground balls, skywalking to snag liners, blasting misplaced fastballs into orbit and generally acting like it was his game and everyone else was there to watch with mouths agape. We could point out his unsustainable BABIP and how his penchant to swing and miss will often keep him from reaching base at an elite rate, but why drop a Baby Ruth in the pool? It was 84 games of beach weather, and then ... ouch. Injuries are part of the game, and there's no reason Tatís shouldn't arrive at spring training with his back in fine fettle. The Padres have asked him to play a little more carefully, which of course they should, but was there any moment watching Tatís last year that made you think he possessed an on/off switch?

YEAR	TEAM	LVL	AGE	PA	DRC+	VORP	BABIP	BRR	FRAA	WARP
2017	FTW	A	18	518	151	52.3	.342	0.1	SS(109): -5.6	4.5
2017	SAN	AA	18	57	70	0.5	.351	0.9	SS(9): -0.3, 3B(3): -0.5	0.0
2018	SAN	AA	19	394	140	35.8	.370	3.0	SS(83): -1.9	3.4
2019	SDN	MLB	20	372	118	26.9	.410	7.1	SS(83): 0.9	3.4
2020	SDN	MLB	21	595	106	33.3	.331	6.1	SS 0	3.4

San Diego Padres 2020

Fernando Tatis Jr., continued

Batted Ball Distribution

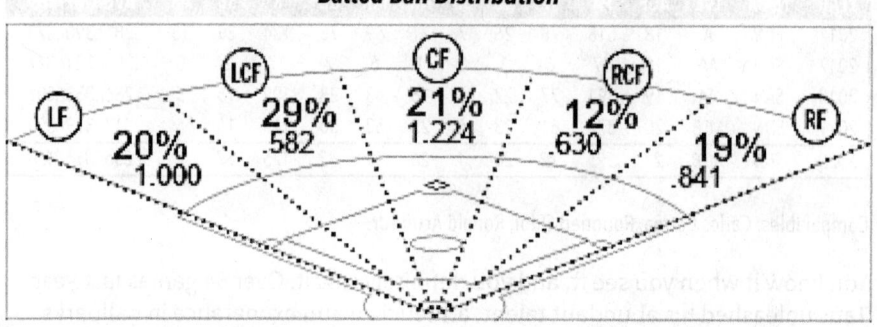

Strike Zone vs LHP

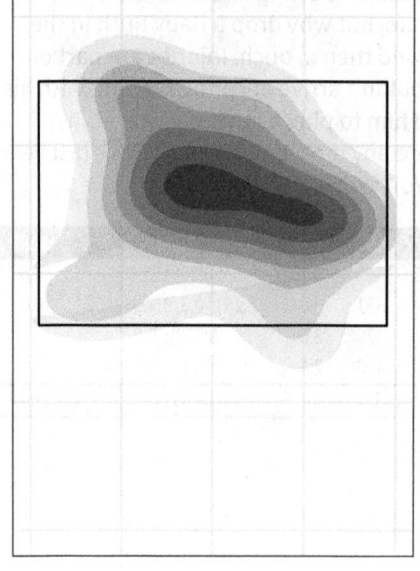

Strike Zone vs RHP

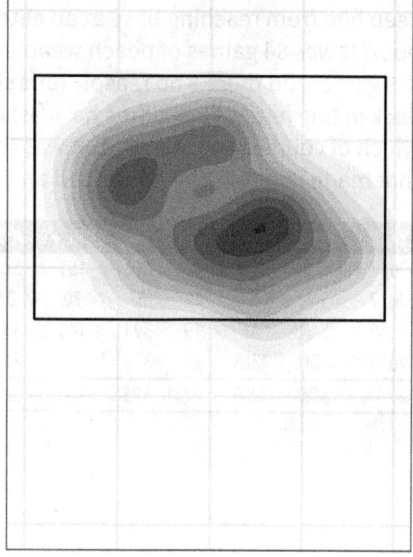

Michel Baez   RHP

Born: 01/21/96   Age: 24   Bats: R   Throws: R
Height: 6'8"   Weight: 220   Origin: International Free Agent, 2016

YEAR	TEAM	LVL	AGE	W	L	SV	G	GS	IP	H	HR	BB/9	K/9	K	GB%	BABIP
2017	FTW	A	21	6	2	0	10	10	58^2	41	8	1.2	12.6	82	36%	.264
2018	LEL	A+	22	4	7	0	17	17	86^2	73	5	3.4	9.6	92	37%	.297
2018	SAN	AA	22	0	3	0	4	4	18^1	22	4	5.9	10.3	21	31%	.375
2019	AMA	AA	23	3	2	1	15	0	27	22	1	3.7	12.7	38	38%	.333
2019	SDN	MLB	23	1	1	0	24	1	29^2	25	3	4.2	8.5	28	40%	.265
2020	SDN	MLB	24	1	2	0	26	8	19	17	3	4.0	8.1	17	38%	.279

Comparables: Jorge Alcala, Vince Velasquez, Ryan Helsley

A *Gran Corona*-sized Cuban signee, Báez unleashed his powerful smoke in the San Diego 'pen last July with encouraging results. His four-seamer sits effortlessly at 96 and Báez supplements it with a solid changeup he can bury for swinging strikes, making it effective against both righties and lefties, though his curveball remains more of a show-me offering. He repeats his delivery surprisingly well for such a big man but will occasionally get out of sync, start issuing walks and lose command. Signed as a starter, Báez worked exclusively in relief last year and flashed late-inning upside but the Padres would be smart to stick him in the rotation to see if his flavor can satisfy all day.

YEAR	TEAM	LVL	AGE	WHIP	ERA	DRA	WARP	MPH	FB%	WHF	CSP
2017	FTW	A	21	0.84	2.45	2.30	2.0				
2018	LEL	A+	22	1.22	2.91	3.01	2.3				
2018	SAN	AA	22	1.85	7.36	7.00	-0.4				
2019	AMA	AA	23	1.22	2.00	3.42	0.4				
2019	SDN	MLB	23	1.31	3.03	5.75	-0.1	97.4	58.7	11.7	41.9
2020	SDN	MLB	24	1.36	4.39	4.57	0.2	97.2	60.5	12.1	43.2

San Diego Padres 2020

Michel Baez, continued

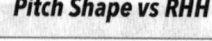
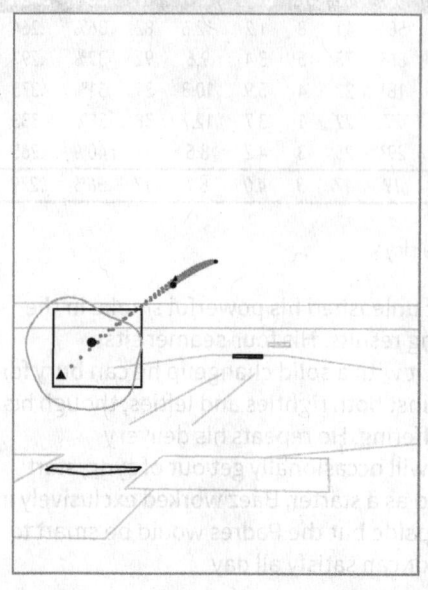
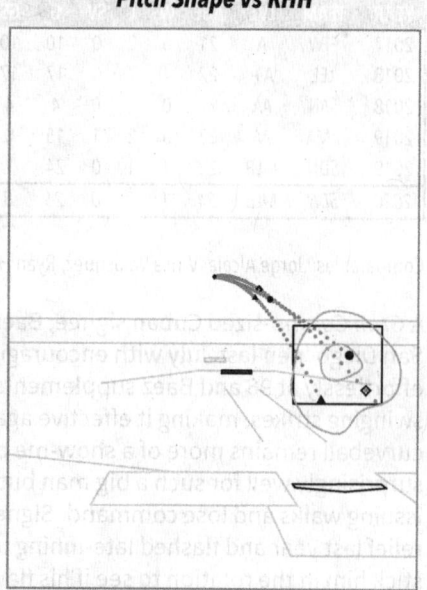

Type	Frequency	Velocity	H Movement	V Movement
● Fastball	58.7%	96.1 [110]	-6.9 [100]	-11.6 [111]
☐ Sinker				
+ Cutter				
▲ Changeup	33.2%	86.1 [103]	-11.7 [97]	-27.3 [100]
✕ Splitter				
▽ Slider				
◇ Curveball	8.1%	82.4 [113]	3.3 [83]	-36.8 [123]
✦ Slow Curveball				
✳ Knuckleball				
▼ Screwball				

Zach Davies RHP

Born: 02/07/93   Age: 27   Bats: R   Throws: R
Height: 6'0"   Weight: 155   Origin: Round 26, 2011 Draft (#785 overall)

YEAR	TEAM	LVL	AGE	W	L	SV	G	GS	IP	H	HR	BB/9	K/9	K	GB%	BABIP
2017	MIL	MLB	24	17	9	0	33	33	191^1	204	20	2.6	5.8	124	51%	.302
2018	WIS	A	25	1	0	0	4	4	19	19	2	0.0	9.0	19	63%	.347
2018	BLX	AA	25	1	1	0	2	2	11	7	1	3.3	9.8	12	54%	.240
2018	CSP	AAA	25	0	3	0	5	5	17	18	0	6.4	6.9	13	44%	.333
2018	MIL	MLB	25	2	7	0	13	13	66	67	8	2.9	6.7	49	48%	.299
2019	MIL	MLB	26	10	7	0	31	31	159^2	155	20	2.9	5.7	102	42%	.272
2020	SDN	MLB	27	7	9	0	24	24	126	130	20	3.0	5.9	84	43%	.281

Comparables: Jair Jurrjens, Art Mahaffey, Joe Ross

Davies continues to thrive as a pitch-to-contact pitcher in a strike-'em-out world. Brett Anderson and Iván Nova were the only starters with a lower strikeout-per-nine rate than Davies' 5.7, but he nonetheless posted the best ERA of his five-year career. (You may have noticed the wide discrepancy between his DRA and ERA—it is indeed one of the biggest in the league among starters.) While Davies will almost certainly not repeat his .272 BABIP from 2019, his lowest in four years by 27 points, his new digs in PETCO Park may just be the best place for a pitcher of his profile. The marine layer promises to keep fly balls from flying out of the yard and the deep power alleys should help Davies feel comfortable continuing to attack the zone and relying on his defense.

YEAR	TEAM	LVL	AGE	WHIP	ERA	DRA	WARP	MPH	FB%	WHF	CSP
2017	MIL	MLB	24	1.35	3.90	4.77	1.7	91.6	57.8	7.6	44.9
2018	WIS	A	25	1.00	2.84	4.71	0.1				
2018	BLX	AA	25	1.00	4.09	3.43	0.2				
2018	CSP	AAA	25	1.76	6.35	5.92	-0.1				
2018	MIL	MLB	25	1.33	4.77	4.68	0.5	92.3	56.5	8.7	43.6
2019	MIL	MLB	26	1.29	3.55	5.30	0.8	90.5	52.4	7.5	41.4
2020	SDN	MLB	27	1.37	4.71	4.93	1.3	90.7	55.5	7.8	43.5

San Diego Padres 2020

Zach Davies, continued

Pitch Shape vs LHH
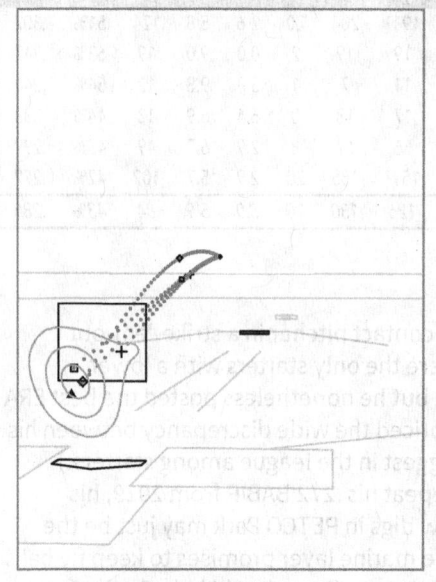

Pitch Shape vs RHH
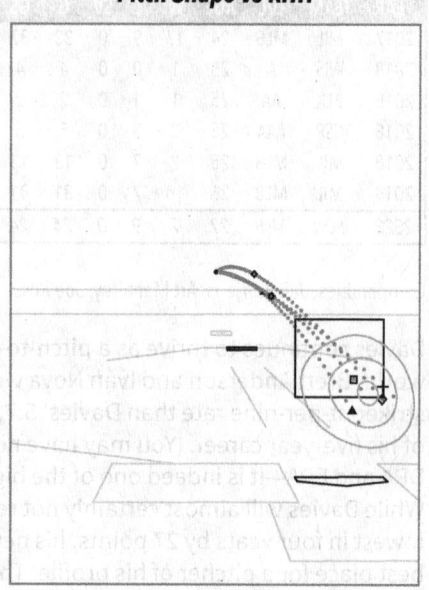

Type	Frequency	Velocity	H Movement	V Movement
● Fastball				
☐ Sinker	52.4%	88.8 [80]	-13.6 [94]	-19.8 [102]
+ Cutter	12.0%	87.2 [91]	-3.6 [68]	-20.7 [113]
▲ Changeup	31.4%	80.3 [82]	-12.8 [92]	-30.6 [91]
✕ Splitter				
▽ Slider				
◇ Curveball	3.7%	76 [91]	7.9 [102]	-50 [95]
✦ Slow Curveball				
✱ Knuckleball				
▼ Screwball				

Jerad Eickhoff RHP
Born: 07/02/90   Age: 29   Bats: R   Throws: R
Height: 6'4"   Weight: 245   Origin: Round 15, 2011 Draft (#474 overall)

YEAR	TEAM	LVL	AGE	W	L	SV	G	GS	IP	H	HR	BB/9	K/9	K	GB%	BABIP
2017	PHI	MLB	26	4	8	0	24	24	128	142	16	3.7	8.3	118	39%	.328
2018	CLR	A+	27	0	1	0	3	3	9	3	2	4.0	10.0	10	42%	.059
2018	LEH	AAA	27	0	0	0	4	4	18^2	17	1	3.9	4.8	10	52%	.267
2018	PHI	MLB	27	0	1	0	3	1	5^1	10	1	0.0	18.6	11	20%	.643
2019	REA	AA	28	0	1	0	2	2	7^1	8	2	3.7	7.4	6	23%	.300
2019	LEH	AAA	28	3	1	0	4	4	17^1	13	3	4.2	8.3	16	27%	.222
2019	PHI	MLB	28	3	4	1	12	10	58^1	58	18	2.8	7.9	51	38%	.256
2020	*PHI*	*MLB*	*29*	*2*	*2*	*0*	*33*	*0*	*35*	*35*	*7*	*3.0*	*8.1*	*32*	*35%*	*.286*

Comparables: Tyler Duffey, Kevin Gausman, Deck McGuire

For a brief, shining moment, it appeared the tumblers had finally clicked into place for Eickhoff, and the injury demons that plagued him during previous seasons had been exorcised. Five major league starts into 2019, Eickhoff had a glittering 1.50 ERA, with 31 strikeouts in 30 innings. Alas, these five starts were a small sample mirage, and for the third year in a row injury dominated and ruined Eickhoff's season. His brief flirtation with success revolved around a shift away from a fastball that dropped below 90 mph last year and toward a biting, low-80s slider. The stuff is still good enough for Eickhoff to cobble together a decent career, but durability is a significant obstacle.

YEAR	TEAM	LVL	AGE	WHIP	ERA	DRA	WARP	MPH	FB%	WHF	CSP
2017	PHI	MLB	26	1.52	4.71	5.24	0.5	92.5	50.2	9.7	48.4
2018	CLR	A+	27	0.78	3.00	2.82	0.3				
2018	LEH	AAA	27	1.34	2.41	4.30	0.3				
2018	PHI	MLB	27	1.88	6.75	3.07	0.1	92.4	52	19.4	49
2019	REA	AA	28	1.50	9.82	5.82	-0.1				
2019	LEH	AAA	28	1.21	4.67	4.14	0.4				
2019	PHI	MLB	28	1.30	5.71	6.14	-0.3	91.5	39.1	11.7	47.9
2020	*PHI*	*MLB*	*29*	*1.33*	*4.79*	*4.90*	*0.2*	*91.4*	*45.6*	*10.8*	*48.4*

San Diego Padres 2020

Jerad Eickhoff, continued

Pitch Shape vs LHH

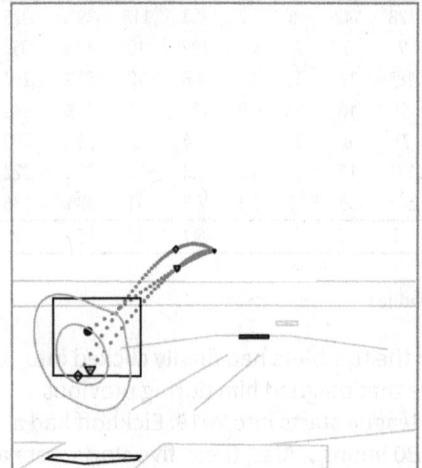

Pitch Shape vs RHH

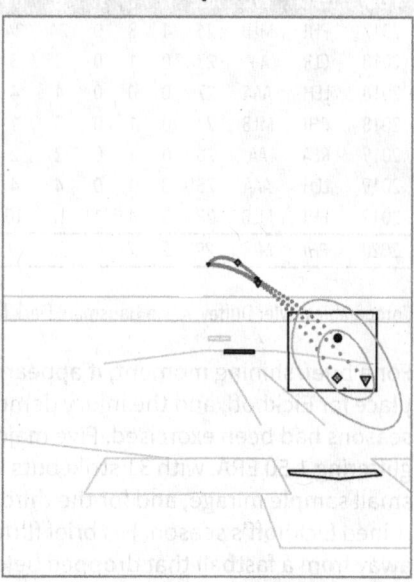

Type	Frequency	Velocity	H Movement	V Movement
● Fastball	38.2%	90 [93]	-7.7 [96]	-14.4 [104]
☐ Sinker				
+ Cutter				
▲ Changeup				
✕ Splitter				
▽ Slider	29.4%	84.4 [100]	0.6 [82]	-28.6 [113]
◇ Curveball	31.5%	75.1 [88]	7.7 [101]	-52.6 [89]
⊕ Slow Curveball				
✳ Knuckleball				
▼ Screwball				

Dinelson Lamet   RHP

Born: 07/18/92   Age: 27   Bats: R   Throws: R
Height: 6'4"   Weight: 187   Origin: International Free Agent, 2014

YEAR	TEAM	LVL	AGE	W	L	SV	G	GS	IP	H	HR	BB/9	K/9	K	GB%	BABIP
2017	ELP	AAA	24	3	2	0	8	8	39	32	2	4.6	11.5	50	52%	.319
2017	SDN	MLB	24	7	8	0	21	21	114[1]	88	18	4.3	10.9	139	37%	.261
2019	LEL	A+	26	0	2	0	3	3	9	11	1	5.0	14.0	14	27%	.476
2019	ELP	AAA	26	1	0	0	3	3	15	10	3	2.4	11.4	19	51%	.219
2019	SDN	MLB	26	3	5	0	14	14	73	62	12	3.7	12.9	105	38%	.311
2020	SDN	MLB	27	8	7	0	23	23	122	99	17	4.1	12.2	166	39%	.299

Comparables: Alex Meyer, Steven Matz, Justin Haley

Tommy John surgery has become so normalized that fans often mark a spot on their mental calendar, assuming the player will reappear unchanged in 18 months, as if they were returning from a 'round-the-world cruise. We often forget the physical and mental challenges they face during long hours spent in anonymous facilities, away from their teammates and the game they love, never sure if their career and livelihood will survive the crisis. Some never make it back at all, some are diminished and some take longer to regain what they've lost. And a handful, like Lamet, return on time, seemingly better than ever. When last we saw the bulldog right-hander, he had mid-90s heat and a wipeout slider, but the lack of a third pitch raised questions about his long-term viability in the rotation. Lamet 2.0, however, has added a tick to his fastball and some variation—a sinking fastball and a slurvy version of his breaking ball—to his repertoire, making it more likely he'll be able to hold his own against lefties and during multiple trips through the order. A healthy Lamet and his heavy dose of sliders will be an asset in the middle of the rotation.

YEAR	TEAM	LVL	AGE	WHIP	ERA	DRA	WARP	MPH	FB%	WHF	CSP
2017	ELP	AAA	24	1.33	3.23	2.42	1.4				
2017	SDN	MLB	24	1.24	4.57	3.97	2.1	97.3	55.8	13	46.6
2019	LEL	A+	26	1.78	8.00	6.22	-0.1				
2019	ELP	AAA	26	0.93	4.80	1.99	0.7				
2019	SDN	MLB	26	1.26	4.07	3.19	2.0	97.9	54.8	14.6	45.9
2020	SDN	MLB	27	1.26	3.79	3.97	2.5	97.1	55.9	14	46.7

San Diego Padres 2020

Dinelson Lamet, continued

Pitch Shape vs LHH	Pitch Shape vs RHH
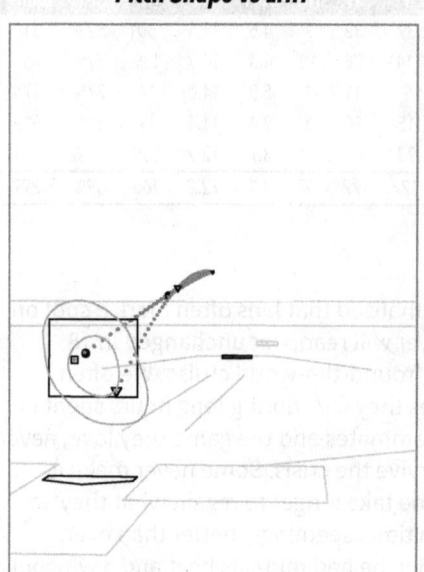	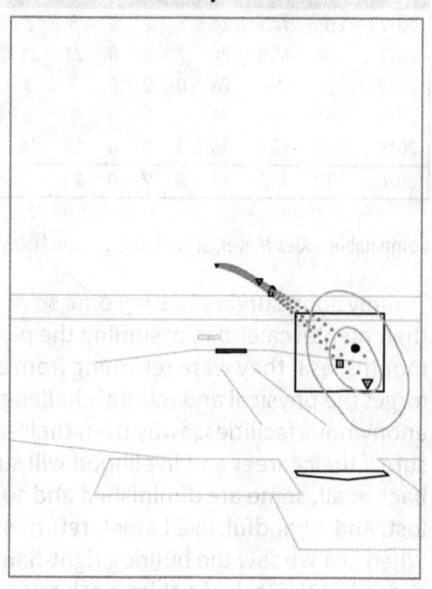

Type	Frequency	Velocity	H Movement	V Movement
● Fastball	37.2%	96 [110]	-4.6 [110]	-12.9 [108]
☐ Sinker	17.5%	96.3 [119]	-11.3 [108]	-14 [122]
+ Cutter				
▲ Changeup				
✕ Splitter				
▽ Slider	43.9%	85.8 [106]	8.1 [113]	-32.9 [100]
◇ Curveball				
✦ Slow Curveball				
✳ Knuckleball				
▼ Screwball				

54 - Padres Player Analysis

Joey Lucchesi   LHP

Born: 06/06/93   Age: 27   Bats: L   Throws: L
Height: 6'5"   Weight: 204   Origin: Round 4, 2016 Draft (#114 overall)

YEAR	TEAM	LVL	AGE	W	L	SV	G	GS	IP	H	HR	BB/9	K/9	K	GB%	BABIP
2017	LEL	A+	24	6	4	0	14	14	78^2	56	9	2.2	10.9	95	53%	.251
2017	SAN	AA	24	5	3	1	10	9	60^1	46	3	2.1	7.9	53	50%	.259
2018	SDN	MLB	25	8	9	0	26	26	130	125	23	3.0	10.0	145	47%	.307
2019	SDN	MLB	26	10	10	0	30	30	163^2	144	23	3.1	8.7	158	49%	.271
2020	SDN	MLB	27	8	8	0	24	24	134	123	22	3.3	9.0	133	47%	.282

Comparables: Trevor Richards, Austin Davis, Brock Stewart

If you want to stick in the rotation as a league-average hurler, as Lucchesi was last summer, it helps to be an interesting one to watch. Old for his draft class and the first pitcher to reach the bigs (Lauer was second), Lucchesi is notable for his wind-up toy delivery, his groovy nickname (Joey Fuego) and his "churve," a changeup-curve hybrid which baffles opposing hitters and pitch classification algorithms with similar frequency. He favors his sinker over his four-seamer and gets his share of groundouts, but isn't a double-play machine. Already set to turn 27 this coming D-Day, Lucchesi isn't a star in waiting but has proven he has both the ability and the durability to munch innings at the back of a big-league rotation.

YEAR	TEAM	LVL	AGE	WHIP	ERA	DRA	WARP	MPH	FB%	WHF	CSP
2017	LEL	A+	24	0.95	2.52	2.73	2.3				
2017	SAN	AA	24	0.99	1.79	2.91	1.6				
2018	SDN	MLB	25	1.29	4.08	3.79	2.3	92.8	64.1	11.5	49.9
2019	SDN	MLB	26	1.22	4.18	4.16	2.9	92.6	64.9	11.5	46.9
2020	SDN	MLB	27	1.29	4.21	4.45	2.0	92.2	65.4	11.6	48.8

San Diego Padres 2020

Joey Lucchesi, continued

Pitch Shape vs LHH

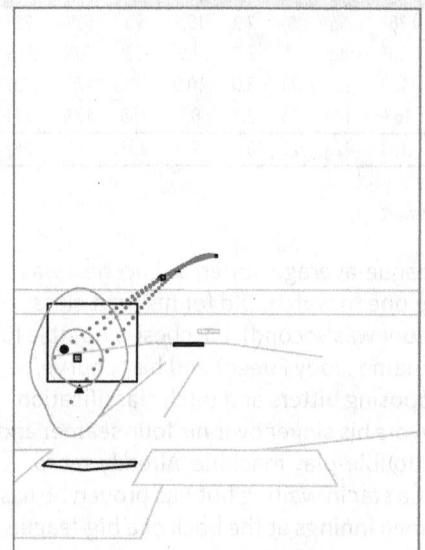

Pitch Shape vs RHH

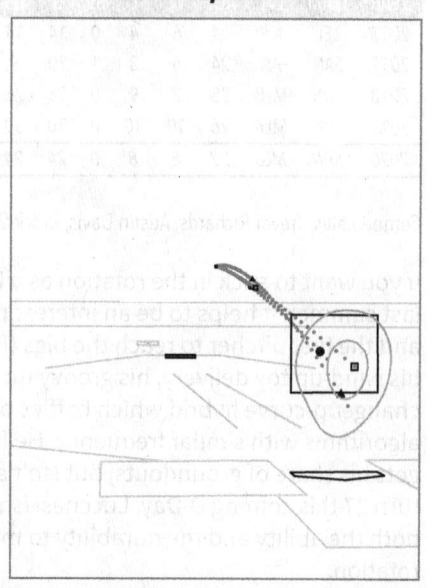

Type	Frequency	Velocity	H Movement	V Movement
● Fastball	14.4%	90.8 [95]	3.2 [116]	-16 [100]
☐ Sinker	50.5%	90.5 [89]	11.1 [110]	-18.2 [108]
+ Cutter				
▲ Changeup	34.1%	79.2 [78]	-0.6 [155]	-38.4 [68]
✕ Splitter				
▽ Slider				
◇ Curveball				
♦ Slow Curveball				
✱ Knuckleball				
▼ Screwball				

Andres Munoz RHP

Born: 01/16/99 Age: 21 Bats: R Throws: R
Height: 6'2" Weight: 165 Origin: International Free Agent, 2015

YEAR	TEAM	LVL	AGE	W	L	SV	G	GS	IP	H	HR	BB/9	K/9	K	GB%	BABIP
2017	TRI	A-	18	3	0	1	21	0	23^2	15	2	6.1	13.3	35	71%	.265
2018	SAN	AA	19	2	1	7	20	0	19	11	0	5.2	9.0	19	55%	.250
2019	AMA	AA	20	0	2	4	16	0	16^2	9	1	5.9	18.4	34	44%	.308
2019	ELP	AAA	20	3	2	2	19	0	19	16	3	3.3	11.4	24	53%	.310
2019	SDN	MLB	20	1	1	1	22	0	23	16	2	4.3	11.7	30	41%	.259
2020	SDN	MLB	21	2	2	2	42	0	45	37	5	4.2	11.9	59	43%	.304

Comparables: Joe Ortiz, Eduardo Sanchez, Mike Soroka

Munoz took the mound to face the Cubs on September 10th sporting a 1.69 ERA and .135/.238/.203 opponents' batting line, testaments to his almighty triple-digit fastball. With a man on, Kris Bryant ambushed a belt-high first-pitch hundo-ball and took Munoz deep for the first time, reminding us all that a misplaced fastball to a big-league hitter is unsafe at any speed. Munoz gave up another dinger to Jason Heyward that day, allowed three more runs in his next appearance and the Padres wisely shut down their fireballing prodigy before his arm and ego were put at further risk. Nevertheless, Munoz was a revelation last year, supplementing his blazing fastball with a sharp-breaking slider he can rush up in the low-90s. Only 21, Munoz has plenty of time to improve his command, take over the ninth inning and perhaps chase down Joakim Soria and Roberto Osuna to set the career saves record for players born in Mexico.

YEAR	TEAM	LVL	AGE	WHIP	ERA	DRA	WARP	MPH	FB%	WHF	CSP
2017	TRI	A-	18	1.31	3.80	3.97	0.3				
2018	SAN	AA	19	1.16	0.95	3.44	0.3				
2019	AMA	AA	20	1.20	2.16	2.06	0.5				
2019	ELP	AAA	20	1.21	3.79	2.91	0.6				
2019	SDN	MLB	20	1.17	3.91	3.98	0.3	101.8	68	15.6	46.1
2020	SDN	MLB	21	1.29	3.77	3.91	0.7	102.0	71.2	16.4	48.3

San Diego Padres 2020

Andres Munoz, continued

Pitch Shape vs LHH	Pitch Shape vs RHH
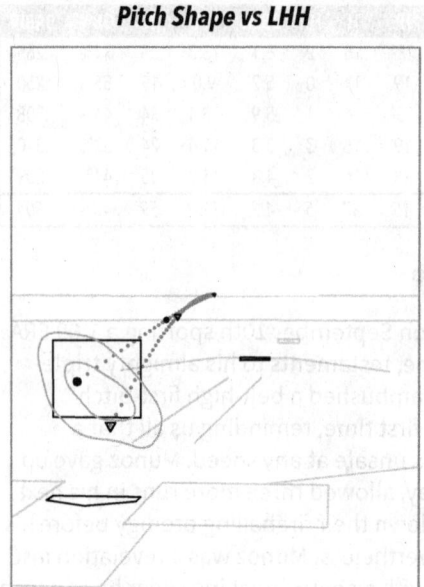	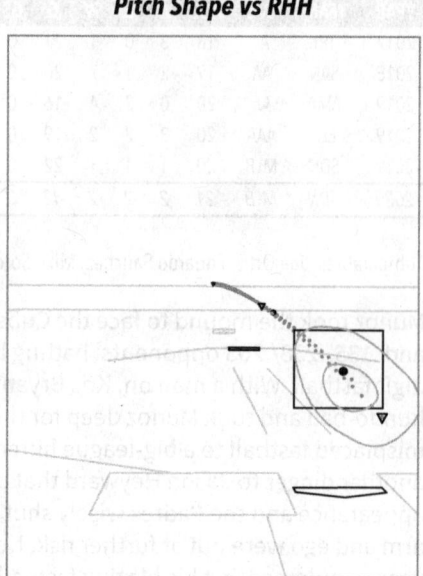

Type	Frequency	Velocity	H Movement	V Movement
● Fastball	67.2%	100.1 [122]	-8.6 [92]	-12.7 [109]
☐ Sinker				
+ Cutter				
▲ Changeup				
✕ Splitter				
▽ Slider	32.0%	86.4 [108]	7.1 [109]	-28.9 [112]
◇ Curveball				
⊕ Slow Curveball				
✳ Knuckleball				
▼ Screwball				

Chris Paddack RHP

Born: 01/08/96   Age: 24   Bats: R   Throws: R
Height: 6'4"   Weight: 195   Origin: Round 8, 2015 Draft (#236 overall)

YEAR	TEAM	LVL	AGE	W	L	SV	G	GS	IP	H	HR	BB/9	K/9	K	GB%	BABIP
2018	LEL	A+	22	4	1	0	10	10	52^1	43	3	0.7	14.3	83	47%	.370
2018	SAN	AA	22	3	2	0	7	7	37^2	23	1	1.0	8.8	37	45%	.239
2019	SDN	MLB	23	9	7	0	26	26	140^2	107	23	2.0	9.8	153	41%	.237
2020	SDN	MLB	24	9	8	0	26	26	143	119	20	2.5	9.5	150	41%	.271

Comparables: Joe Musgrove, Daniel Hudson, Corbin Burnes

Black suit. Black hat. Dark shades. Lone Star boots, trimmed in … baby blue? Pink tie? Under Armour backpack? Mullet? Paddack arrived for his first big-league start sporting his own precocious take on Urban Cowboy, and the kid from suburban Austin ended the year pitching like the latest big thing from Texas. In between, Paddack displayed the confidence and tenacity that helped him return from Tommy John surgery, catapult up prospect lists and succeed in The Show after only 33 minor-league starts, and his strong finish after a mid-season slump speaks well of his ability to adjust on the fly. Paddack's fastball sits in the mid 90s and he commands it well, painting the black or drawing empty swings high out of the zone, while his changeup already ranks among the best in the game. Continued development of his inconsistent curveball may be the difference between Paddack becoming a true ace or a solid second starter, and this year there will be no innings restrictions to hold him back—just wide open skies, bluebonnet hillsides and a burble of ZZ Top floating on the breeze.

YEAR	TEAM	LVL	AGE	WHIP	ERA	DRA	WARP	MPH	FB%	WHF	CSP
2018	LEL	A+	22	0.90	2.24	2.22	1.9				
2018	SAN	AA	22	0.72	1.91	2.09	1.4				
2019	SDN	MLB	23	0.98	3.33	3.18	4.0	96.2	61	12.9	50.5
2020	SDN	MLB	24	1.11	3.34	3.63	3.4	96.0	62.9	13.3	52

San Diego Padres 2020

Chris Paddack, continued

Pitch Shape vs LHH

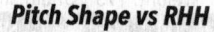

Pitch Shape vs RHH

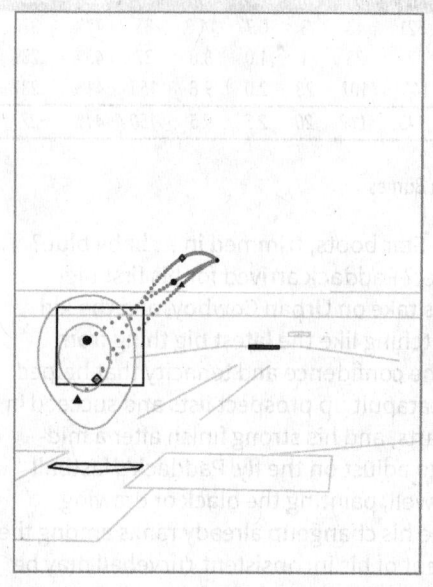

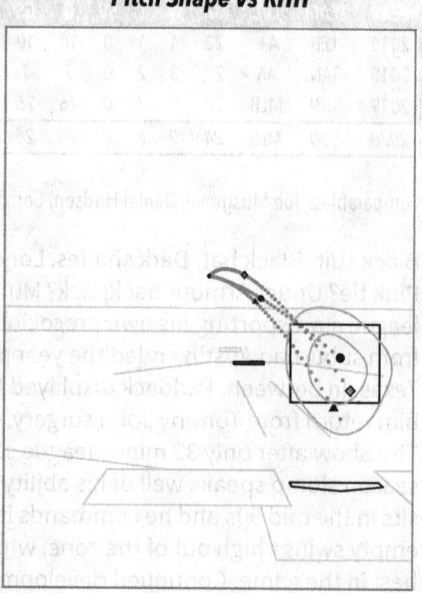

Type	Frequency	Velocity	H Movement	V Movement
● Fastball	61.0%	94.2 [105]	-6.3 [103]	-11.3 [112]
☐ Sinker				
+ Cutter				
▲ Changeup	28.5%	84.8 [98]	-10.1 [105]	-26 [104]
✕ Splitter				
▽ Slider				
◇ Curveball	10.4%	76.4 [93]	6.2 [95]	-53.6 [87]
◈ Slow Curveball				
✳ Knuckleball				
▼ Screwball				

60 - Padres Player Analysis

Emilio Pagán RHP

Born: 05/07/91   Age: 29   Bats: L   Throws: R
Height: 6'3"   Weight: 205   Origin: Round 10, 2013 Draft (#297 overall)

YEAR	TEAM	LVL	AGE	W	L	SV	G	GS	IP	H	HR	BB/9	K/9	K	GB%	BABIP
2017	TAC	AAA	26	2	1	5	23	0	31[2]	19	0	2.3	10.2	36	29%	.241
2017	SEA	MLB	26	2	3	0	34	0	50[1]	39	7	1.4	10.0	56	23%	.258
2018	NAS	AAA	27	1	0	0	5	0	6	5	2	0.0	16.5	11	38%	.273
2018	OAK	MLB	27	3	1	0	55	0	62	55	13	2.8	9.1	63	25%	.256
2019	DUR	AAA	28	0	0	2	4	1	6	2	0	6.0	15.0	10	46%	.182
2019	TBA	MLB	28	4	2	20	66	0	70	45	12	1.7	12.3	96	35%	.228
2020	TBA	MLB	29	3	2	22	48	0	51	39	8	2.6	12.0	68	32%	.276

Comparables: Paul Sewald, Richard Rodríguez, Ryan Garton

Pagán did not make the Rays' Opening Day roster after losing the final spot to Adam Kolarek. By the end of the season, Kolarek was pitching in Los Angeles and Pagán was Tampa Bay's closer. It goes that way sometimes. Part of Pagán's ascent into the high-leverage life had to do with the failure of others. Jose Alvarado struggled as the closer and the committee approach was not much better. By the time the club acquired Nick Anderson, Pagán had established himself as a reliable reliever and allowed Anderson's fresh arm to get big outs in the seventh and eighth innings. A prototypical two-pitch reliever, Pagán got most of his outs with either a fastball or a slider. As a fly-ball pitcher, he can sometimes give up the big one, but he limits traffic on the bases with an elite walk rate. Anderson and Castillo are better pitchers, but Pagán won't sweat that little detail if he converts more saves and cashes those eventual arb-year checks.

YEAR	TEAM	LVL	AGE	WHIP	ERA	DRA	WARP	MPH	FB%	WHF	CSP
2017	TAC	AAA	26	0.85	2.56	1.55	1.3				
2017	SEA	MLB	26	0.93	3.22	3.68	0.8	95.8	68.7	15	54.7
2018	NAS	AAA	27	0.83	3.00	1.98	0.2				
2018	OAK	MLB	27	1.19	4.35	4.35	0.4	96.1	66.4	15.5	50.9
2019	DUR	AAA	28	1.00	0.00	1.74	0.3				
2019	TBA	MLB	28	0.83	2.31	2.91	1.9	97.4	61.5	19.3	50.2
2020	TBA	MLB	29	1.05	2.88	3.27	1.1	96.0	64.5	17.2	51.6

San Diego Padres 2020

Emilio Pagán, continued

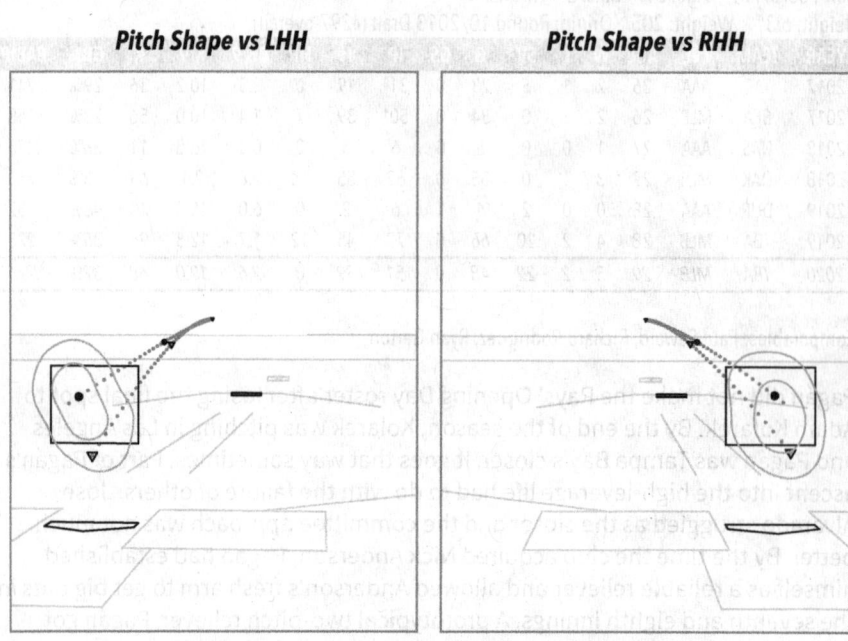

Type	Frequency	Velocity	H Movement	V Movement
● Fastball	61.5%	95.9 [110]	-4.1 [112]	-10.6 [114]
☐ Sinker				
+ Cutter				
▲ Changeup				
✕ Splitter				
▽ Slider	36.4%	88 [115]	3.2 [93]	-28.4 [114]
◇ Curveball				
◈ Slow Curveball				
✳ Knuckleball				
▼ Screwball				

Luis Perdomo   RHP

Born: 05/09/93   Age: 27   Bats: R   Throws: R
Height: 6'2"   Weight: 185   Origin: International Free Agent, 2003

YEAR	TEAM	LVL	AGE	W	L	SV	G	GS	IP	H	HR	BB/9	K/9	K	GB%	BABIP
2017	SDN	MLB	24	8	11	0	29	29	163^2	182	17	3.6	6.5	118	62%	.325
2018	ELP	AAA	25	6	3	0	13	13	75	72	12	2.5	7.3	61	57%	.284
2018	SDN	MLB	25	1	6	0	12	10	44^2	62	4	4.4	7.9	39	44%	.389
2019	ELP	AAA	26	2	1	1	11	0	15	21	3	2.4	10.2	17	53%	.409
2019	SDN	MLB	26	2	4	0	47	1	72	69	6	2.2	6.9	55	54%	.298
2020	SDN	MLB	27	3	3	0	60	0	64	67	8	3.1	7.6	54	54%	.310

Comparables: Jose Acevedo, James Baldwin, Jakob Junis

The Padres' commitment to the kiddie corps in their rotation sent Old Man Perdomo to the 'pen last year, with perfectly acceptable and mostly forgettable results. His sinker-slider mix featured less of the former and more of the latter, and while his stuff didn't exactly bloom, Perdomo showed improved command in shorter stints. He threw more strikes, cut his walk rate and continued to induce plenty of ground balls, providing his manager with a reliable multi-inning option to clean up someone else's messy start. His future as a mid-rotation stalwart has flown north with the butterflies, but Perdomo can take comfort from the fact that every bullpen needs a janitor.

YEAR	TEAM	LVL	AGE	WHIP	ERA	DRA	WARP	MPH	FB%	WHF	CSP
2017	SDN	MLB	24	1.51	4.67	4.96	1.1	96.3	62.8	9.6	47.1
2018	ELP	AAA	25	1.24	3.72	3.38	1.8				
2018	SDN	MLB	25	1.88	7.05	6.52	-0.6	95.6	63	8	47.1
2019	ELP	AAA	26	1.67	3.60	5.04	0.2				
2019	SDN	MLB	26	1.21	4.00	4.31	0.8	95.8	54.5	9.6	49.4
2020	SDN	MLB	27	1.40	4.59	4.69	0.5	95.5	60.9	9.4	48.6

San Diego Padres 2020

Luis Perdomo, continued

Pitch Shape vs LHH

Pitch Shape vs RHH

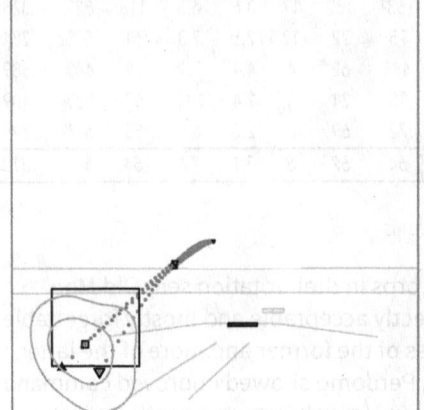
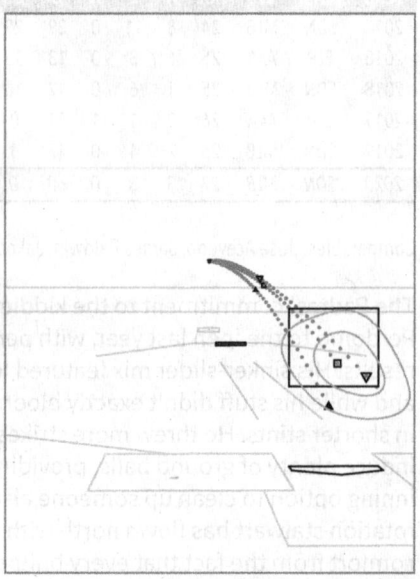

Type	Frequency	Velocity	H Movement	V Movement
● Fastball				
☐ Sinker	51.7%	94.3 [109]	-12.7 [100]	-18.9 [105]
+ Cutter				
▲ Changeup	11.1%	88.5 [112]	-12.2 [95]	-26.8 [102]
✕ Splitter				
▽ Slider	34.5%	86.8 [110]	1.5 [85]	-32 [103]
◇ Curveball				
✦ Slow Curveball				
✱ Knuckleball				
▼ Screwball				

Drew Pomeranz LHP

Born: 11/22/88 Age: 31 Bats: R Throws: L
Height: 6'6" Weight: 240 Origin: Round 1, 2010 Draft (#5 overall)

YEAR	TEAM	LVL	AGE	W	L	SV	G	GS	IP	H	HR	BB/9	K/9	K	GB%	BABIP
2017	BOS	MLB	28	17	6	0	32	32	173^2	166	19	3.6	9.0	174	45%	.310
2018	PAW	AAA	29	0	2	0	5	5	19^2	16	7	5.9	5.5	12	58%	.173
2018	BOS	MLB	29	2	6	0	26	11	74	87	12	5.4	8.0	66	39%	.344
2019	MIL	MLB	30	0	1	2	25	1	26^1	16	4	2.7	15.4	45	47%	.279
2019	SFN	MLB	30	2	9	0	21	17	77^2	89	17	4.2	10.7	92	39%	.350
2020	SDN	MLB	31	3	3	4	60	0	64	59	9	3.9	10.5	75	41%	.306

Comparables: Danny Duffy, Brian Matusz, Andrew Miller

Starting just isn't for Pomeranz. After another 17 mediocre starts for the Giants (and one spot-start following his midseason trade to Milwaukee), his career ERA in the role was 4.25. The sample size is much smaller for Pomeranz in the bullpen, but he has a career 2.72 ERA (and .596 OPS allowed) in 102 career relief appearances. The velocity increase out of the pen for Pomeranz tells much of the story—his average fastball rose from roughly 92 mph in the season's early months to 95-plus as in August and September. He leaned into it more, too, letting it eat. The Padres believed in Pomeranz's relief dominance enough to hand him a four-year deal worth $34 million.

YEAR	TEAM	LVL	AGE	WHIP	ERA	DRA	WARP	MPH	FB%	WHF	CSP
2017	BOS	MLB	28	1.35	3.32	4.17	2.7	93.8	61.6	10.6	43.1
2018	PAW	AAA	29	1.47	5.49	5.25	0.1				
2018	BOS	MLB	29	1.77	6.08	7.90	-2.3	91.8	58.9	7.9	43.7
2019	MIL	MLB	30	0.91	2.39	0.00	1.6	96.2	63.8	19.5	48.7
2019	SFN	MLB	30	1.61	5.68	5.91	-0.2	94.5	63.8	10.4	48.8
2020	SDN	MLB	31	1.36	4.30	4.45	0.7	93.0	61.4	10.6	45.4

San Diego Padres 2020

Drew Pomeranz, continued

Pitch Shape vs LHH   Pitch Shape vs RHH

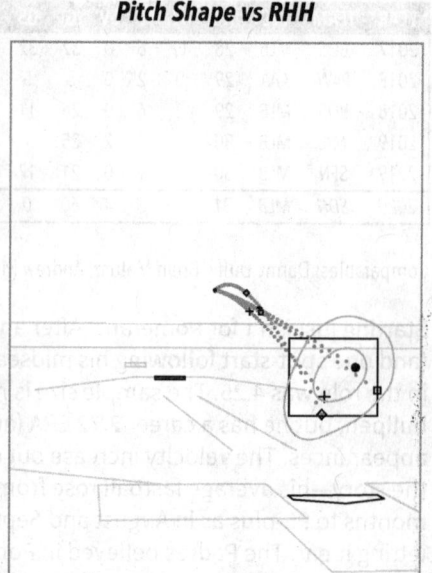

Type	Frequency	Velocity	H Movement	V Movement
● Fastball	54.7%	93 [102]	5.6 [106]	-11.7 [111]
☐ Sinker	6.2%	91.3 [93]	12.1 [103]	-16.3 [114]
+ Cutter	5.7%	88.3 [98]	-0.3 [91]	-20.4 [114]
▲ Changeup				
✕ Splitter				
▽ Slider				
◇ Curveball	31.9%	81.4 [109]	-2.5 [80]	-49.9 [95]
⊕ Slow Curveball				
✻ Knuckleball				
▼ Screwball				

Cal Quantrill   RHP
Born: 02/10/95   Age: 25   Bats: L   Throws: R
Height: 6'3"   Weight: 208   Origin: Round 1, 2016 Draft (#8 overall)

YEAR	TEAM	LVL	AGE	W	L	SV	G	GS	IP	H	HR	BB/9	K/9	K	GB%	BABIP
2017	LEL	A+	22	6	5	0	14	14	73^2	78	5	2.9	9.3	76	42%	.353
2017	SAN	AA	22	1	5	0	8	8	42^1	52	5	3.4	7.2	34	39%	.341
2018	SAN	AA	23	6	5	0	22	22	117	135	12	2.9	7.8	101	45%	.336
2018	ELP	AAA	23	3	1	0	6	6	31	39	4	1.5	6.4	22	50%	.333
2019	ELP	AAA	24	4	2	0	7	7	35^2	38	3	3.0	8.3	33	52%	.324
2019	SDN	MLB	24	6	8	0	23	18	103	106	15	2.4	7.8	89	45%	.295
2020	SDN	MLB	25	4	4	0	28	10	70	68	10	2.9	7.5	58	45%	.285

Comparables: Mike Mayers, Mike Wright, Trevor Williams

Quantrill's performance has consistently lagged behind his raw stuff and pedigree, ever since the Padres made him the eighth-overall pick in 2016, and his first spin through the senior circuit was more of the same. On the plus side, righties continually pounded his mid-90s fastball and sinker into the ground and swung through his slider and changeup en route to a miniscule .217/.243/.337 line with a 44:6 whiff-to-walk ratio. Unfortunately for Quantrill, his once-vaunted changeup did nothing to stop lefties from staging a nightly laser show. He doesn't have a true wipeout offering, but he keeps his walks in check, and if Quantrill can leverage some sort of voodoo to tame the lefties that have tortured him, he might be able to survive at the end of the rotation.

YEAR	TEAM	LVL	AGE	WHIP	ERA	DRA	WARP	MPH	FB%	WHF	CSP
2017	LEL	A+	22	1.38	3.67	4.85	0.4				
2017	SAN	AA	22	1.61	4.04	6.11	-0.5				
2018	SAN	AA	23	1.48	5.15	5.74	-0.5				
2018	ELP	AAA	23	1.42	3.48	4.56	0.3				
2019	ELP	AAA	24	1.40	4.54	3.78	1.0				
2019	SDN	MLB	24	1.30	5.16	4.34	1.5	96.2	56.7	10.8	44.6
2020	SDN	MLB	25	1.29	4.20	4.45	1.0	95.9	58.1	11.1	45.7

San Diego Padres 2020

Cal Quantrill, continued

Pitch Shape vs LHH

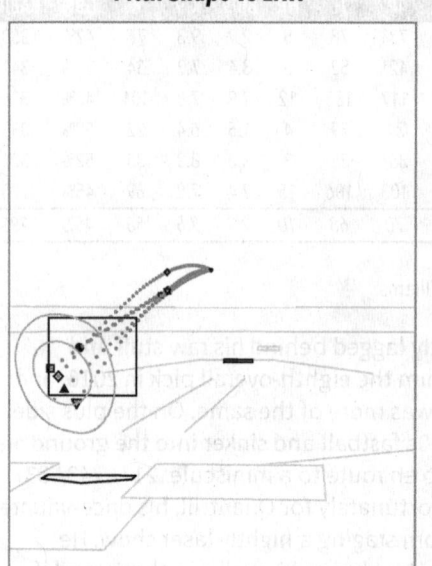

Pitch Shape vs RHH

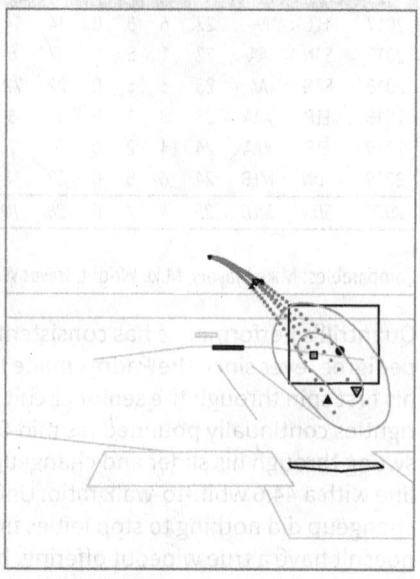

Type	Frequency	Velocity	H Movement	V Movement
● Fastball	22.4%	94.7 [107]	-7.1 [99]	-12.9 [108]
□ Sinker	34.3%	94.5 [110]	-12.1 [104]	-15.6 [117]
+ Cutter				
▲ Changeup	18.1%	84.9 [99]	-7.1 [119]	-24 [110]
✕ Splitter				
▽ Slider	21.2%	86.6 [109]	3.3 [93]	-30.7 [107]
◇ Curveball	3.9%	79.5 [103]	3.6 [84]	-41.8 [112]
✥ Slow Curveball				
✳ Knuckleball				
▼ Screwball				

Gerardo Reyes RHP

Born: 05/13/93   Age: 27   Bats: R   Throws: R
Height: 5'11"   Weight: 160   Origin: Undrafted Free Agent, 2013

YEAR	TEAM	LVL	AGE	W	L	SV	G	GS	IP	H	HR	BB/9	K/9	K	GB%	BABIP
2017	LEL	A+	24	3	3	5	47	0	61^2	54	3	4.5	9.5	65	51%	.317
2018	LEL	A+	25	0	1	1	14	0	16^1	11	0	6.6	11.0	20	43%	.297
2018	SAN	AA	25	1	2	1	31	0	39	32	1	3.9	11.3	49	39%	.323
2019	ELP	AAA	26	4	2	3	34	0	45^1	39	8	4.0	12.1	61	35%	.310
2019	SDN	MLB	26	4	0	0	27	0	26	24	3	3.8	13.2	38	40%	.339
2020	SDN	MLB	27	2	2	0	36	0	38	31	5	4.3	12.4	52	37%	.299

Comparables: Colton Murray, Brandon Cunniff, Ryan Garton

Yet another San Diego bullpen centurion, Reyes is a joy to watch as he uncoils his short, slight frame and unleashes upper-90s heat from a sidearm slot with a windmill kick finish. When he's on, he fills the zone, and opposing righties have no chance to pick up the spin of his slider or catch up to his fastball; when he's off, he walks the yard and lefties take him to the woodshed. Reyes shuttled between El Paso and San Diego a half-dozen times last year and he never found a consistent groove, but the Padres will likely give the once-anonymous free agent from Galveston College every chance to make a name for himself in middle relief.

YEAR	TEAM	LVL	AGE	WHIP	ERA	DRA	WARP	MPH	FB%	WHF	CSP
2017	LEL	A+	24	1.38	2.63	4.02	0.6				
2018	LEL	A+	25	1.41	2.20	3.30	0.3				
2018	SAN	AA	25	1.26	3.00	3.59	0.6				
2019	ELP	AAA	26	1.30	3.57	3.56	1.2				
2019	SDN	MLB	26	1.35	7.62	3.30	0.6	99.0	73.6	18.1	48.6
2020	SDN	MLB	27	1.28	3.95	4.08	0.6	98.5	74.5	18.3	49.2

San Diego Padres 2020

Gerardo Reyes, continued

Pitch Shape vs LHH	Pitch Shape vs RHH
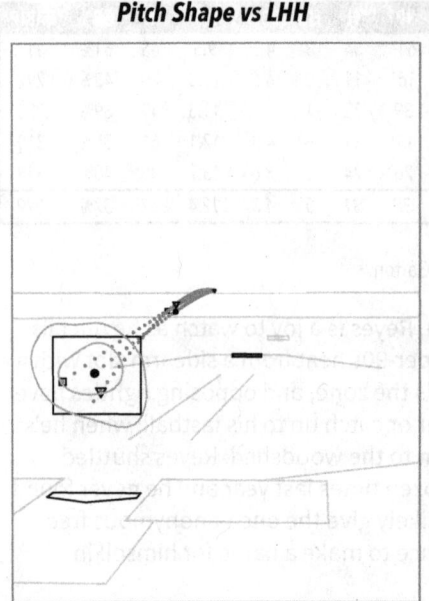	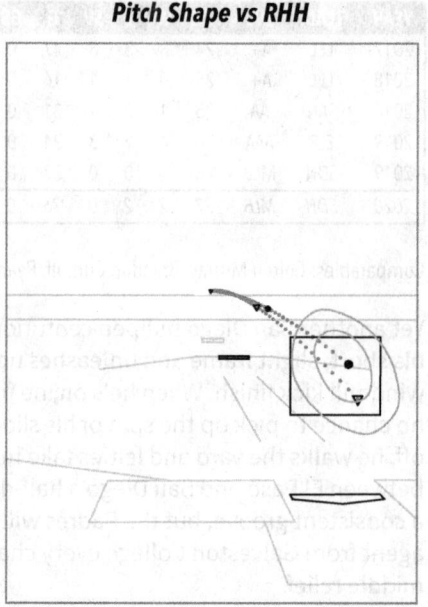

Type	Frequency	Velocity	H Movement	V Movement
● Fastball	56.1%	97.1 [113]	-9 [90]	-14.9 [103]
☐ Sinker	17.5%	97 [123]	-14.5 [88]	-20.4 [100]
+ Cutter				
▲ Changeup				
✕ Splitter				
▽ Slider	26.4%	87.9 [115]	2.1 [88]	-29.3 [111]
◇ Curveball				
✦ Slow Curveball				
✱ Knuckleball				
▼ Screwball				

Garrett Richards RHP

Born: 05/27/88 Age: 32 Bats: R Throws: R
Height: 6'3" Weight: 210 Origin: Round 1, 2009 Draft (#42 overall)

YEAR	TEAM	LVL	AGE	W	L	SV	G	GS	IP	H	HR	BB/9	K/9	K	GB%	BABIP
2017	LAA	MLB	29	0	2	0	6	6	27^2	18	1	2.3	8.8	27	55%	.233
2018	LAA	MLB	30	5	4	0	16	16	76^1	64	11	4.0	10.3	87	50%	.277
2019	LEL	A+	31	0	1	0	3	3	6^2	8	1	10.8	10.8	8	47%	.389
2019	SDN	MLB	31	0	1	0	3	3	8^2	10	2	6.2	11.4	11	46%	.364
2020	SDN	MLB	32	8	8	0	24	24	134	116	16	3.7	9.9	147	46%	.291

Comparables: Tyson Ross, Bob Gibson, Andrew Cashner

The Padres signed Richards to a two-year, $15.5 million contract prior to last season, expecting the long-time, oft-injured Angels star to miss all of 2019 recovering from Tommy John surgery. That Richards was able to make three big-league starts was a bonus; that he struggled mightily with his control was unsurprising. The important thing is, his estimable stuff—a heavy mid-90s fastball, hard slider and usable curve—seems to have survived the knife. The idea has always been for Richards to return in 2020 and provide veteran leadership to the young Padres rotation, and with a normal offseason to regain his command and stretch out his arm, he'll likely post above-average numbers. That is, if he's healthy. Having lost most of the last four seasons to injury, that will always be the question with Richards.

YEAR	TEAM	LVL	AGE	WHIP	ERA	DRA	WARP	MPH	FB%	WHF	CSP
2017	LAA	MLB	29	0.90	2.28	3.12	0.8	97.5	58.2	13.2	43.8
2018	LAA	MLB	30	1.28	3.66	3.73	1.4	97.8	50.4	12.3	47.5
2019	LEL	A+	31	2.40	8.10	8.95	-0.3				
2019	SDN	MLB	31	1.85	8.31	3.75	0.2	96.3	58	11.5	45
2020	SDN	MLB	32	1.28	3.81	3.98	2.7	96.6	52.1	12.2	45.1

San Diego Padres 2020

Garrett Richards, continued

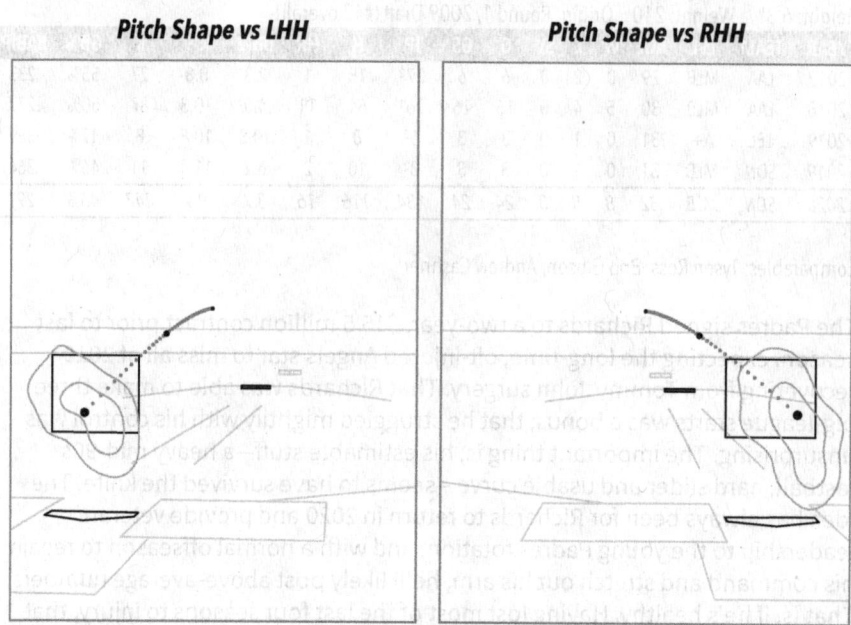

Type	Frequency	Velocity	H Movement	V Movement
● Fastball	47.1%	95 [107]	0.4 [132]	-18.6 [93]
□ Sinker	10.8%	95.8 [116]	-7.9 [131]	-18.7 [106]
+ Cutter				
▲ Changeup				
✕ Splitter				
▽ Slider	29.3%	89.2 [120]	2.8 [91]	-33.2 [100]
◇ Curveball	12.1%	80.5 [106]	11.3 [115]	-57 [80]
✦ Slow Curveball				
✱ Knuckleball				
▼ Screwball				

Craig Stammen   RHP

Born: 03/09/84   Age: 36   Bats: R   Throws: R
Height: 6'4"   Weight: 230   Origin: Round 12, 2005 Draft (#354 overall)

YEAR	TEAM	LVL	AGE	W	L	SV	G	GS	IP	H	HR	BB/9	K/9	K	GB%	BABIP
2017	SDN	MLB	33	2	3	0	60	0	80[1]	68	12	3.1	8.3	74	52%	.263
2018	SDN	MLB	34	8	3	0	73	0	79	65	3	1.9	10.0	88	51%	.301
2019	SDN	MLB	35	8	7	4	76	0	82	80	13	1.6	8.0	73	51%	.284
2020	SDN	MLB	36	3	3	0	60	0	64	58	8	2.3	8.3	59	51%	.282

Comparables: Matt Belisle, Chad Qualls, Tim Worrell

Middle relievers live and die by the vagaries of small sample sizes. A starter may struggle through 60 tough innings in April and May, but have the luxury of four more months to right the ship. For a middle reliever, those 60 innings are the full season on which you're judged and eventually compensated. That's what makes Stammen's ability to churn out 80-inning, 3.00 ERA, 1.2 WHIP seasons year after year after year so rare and valuable. His fastball/sinker/slider/curve repertoire is unremarkable, but he throws strikes, generates ground balls and keeps his teammates in games. There are a few warning signs, as Stammen is entering his late thirties with a swinging strike rate that has dropped below 10 percent for the first time in a decade, but betting against him still feels like betting against the sun rising.

YEAR	TEAM	LVL	AGE	WHIP	ERA	DRA	WARP	MPH	FB%	WHF	CSP
2017	SDN	MLB	33	1.20	3.14	3.76	1.3	93.3	63.3	12.2	44.1
2018	SDN	MLB	34	1.04	2.73	2.86	1.9	94.0	67.6	14.6	47
2019	SDN	MLB	35	1.16	3.29	4.27	1.0	94.6	72.2	9.8	46
2020	SDN	MLB	36	1.16	3.44	3.74	1.2	92.8	67	11.7	44.9

San Diego Padres 2020

Craig Stammen, continued

Pitch Shape vs LHH
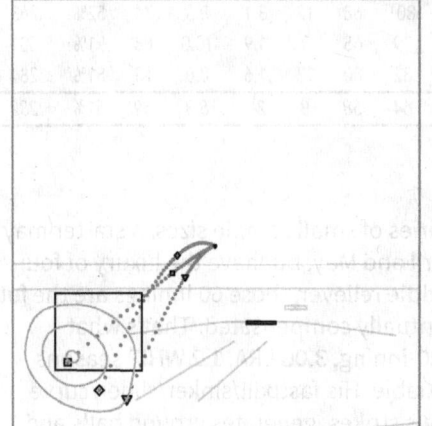

Pitch Shape vs RHH
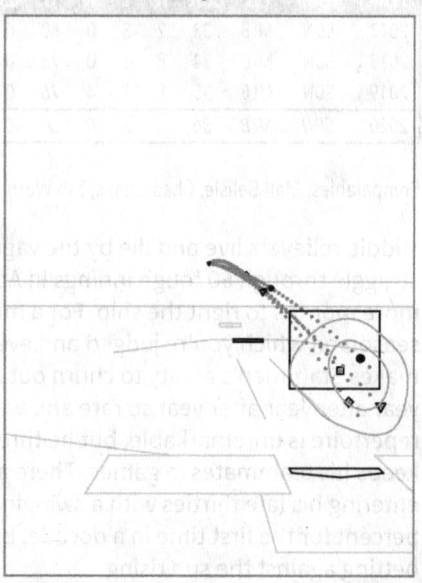

Type	Frequency	Velocity	H Movement	V Movement
● Fastball	4.7%	92.7 [101]	-11.1 [81]	-16.4 [99]
☐ Sinker	67.5%	93.1 [103]	-12.5 [101]	-18.9 [105]
+ Cutter				
▲ Changeup				
✗ Splitter				
▽ Slider	15.7%	87.8 [114]	2.4 [89]	-27.5 [116]
◇ Curveball	12.0%	81.6 [110]	7.4 [100]	-47.6 [100]
✦ Slow Curveball				
✱ Knuckleball				
▼ Screwball				

Matt Strahm LHP

Born: 11/12/91   Age: 28   Bats: R   Throws: L
Height: 6'3"   Weight: 185   Origin: Round 21, 2012 Draft (#643 overall)

YEAR	TEAM	LVL	AGE	W	L	SV	G	GS	IP	H	HR	BB/9	K/9	K	GB%	BABIP
2017	KCA	MLB	25	2	5	0	24	3	34^2	30	6	5.7	9.6	37	42%	.279
2018	SAN	AA	26	1	0	0	9	2	14^1	14	1	2.5	13.8	22	42%	.406
2018	SDN	MLB	26	3	4	0	41	5	61^1	39	6	3.1	10.1	69	37%	.226
2019	SDN	MLB	27	6	11	0	46	16	114^2	121	22	1.7	9.3	118	38%	.308
2020	SDN	MLB	28	2	2	0	48	0	51	45	8	2.5	9.2	52	38%	.276

Comparables: Hansel Robles, Brock Stewart, Mike Clevinger

Strahm struggled out of the gate in the San Diego rotation but once again proved electric in a relief role. After moving to the 'pen lefties were doomed when he was on the mound, posting a .137/.185/.294 line, and overall, batters lost 200 points of OPS facing PenStrahm compared to StartStrahm. The lean, leonine lefty possesses a broad four-pitch mix, but his stuff plays up in shorter stints and with certain matchups, making it likely his future lies in relief. It remains a bright one.

YEAR	TEAM	LVL	AGE	WHIP	ERA	DRA	WARP	MPH	FB%	WHF	CSP
2017	KCA	MLB	25	1.50	5.45	5.80	-0.2	96.1	67.3	11.2	49.1
2018	SAN	AA	26	1.26	2.51	3.11	0.3				
2018	SDN	MLB	26	0.98	2.05	3.96	0.7	96.0	58	13.3	52.9
2019	SDN	MLB	27	1.25	4.71	4.29	1.7	94.0	38.2	11.8	53.9
2020	SDN	MLB	28	1.16	3.77	4.06	0.8	94.2	47.7	12.2	52.7

San Diego Padres 2020

Matt Strahm, continued

Pitch Shape vs LHH   Pitch Shape vs RHH

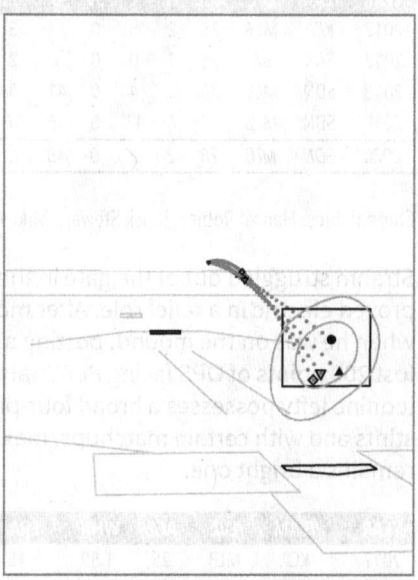

Type	Frequency	Velocity	H Movement	V Movement
● Fastball	38.1%	91.8 [98]	12.9 [73]	-17.8 [95]
☐ Sinker				
+ Cutter				
▲ Changeup	13.9%	84.6 [98]	16.2 [77]	-30.9 [90]
✕ Splitter				
▽ Slider	31.2%	86.2 [107]	-2 [88]	-26.4 [119]
◇ Curveball	16.8%	80.2 [105]	-6.2 [95]	-38.2 [120]
⊕ Slow Curveball				
✱ Knuckleball				
▼ Screwball				

Adam Warren   RHP

Born: 08/25/87   Age: 32   Bats: R   Throws: R
Height: 6'1"   Weight: 224   Origin: Round 4, 2009 Draft (#135 overall)

YEAR	TEAM	LVL	AGE	W	L	SV	G	GS	IP	H	HR	BB/9	K/9	K	GB%	BABIP
2017	NYA	MLB	29	3	2	1	46	0	57^1	35	4	2.4	8.5	54	44%	.208
2018	NYA	MLB	30	0	1	0	24	0	30	26	3	3.6	11.1	37	37%	.307
2018	SEA	MLB	30	3	1	0	23	0	21^2	22	3	3.3	6.2	15	39%	.279
2019	SDN	MLB	31	4	1	0	25	0	28^2	28	9	3.8	7.8	25	44%	.247
2020	NYA	MLB	32	2	2	0	33	0	35	34	6	3.7	8.1	31	42%	.281

Comparables: Jeremy Jeffress, David Phelps, Ramon E Ramirez

Last year in this space we posited a wild theory that Warren's suckitude in any uniform other than Yankee pinstripes was due to a sinister plot involving androids. This year, we're lowering the android threat level from "Hmmmmm" to "Yeah, right," as Warren's most recent west coast clunker ended after 29 innings (and nine home runs) when his elbow went *sproing*. Tommy John surgery ensued in September, and Warren will likely be out until the 2021 season. Androids don't have elbow ligaments, of course. Or do they? Hmmmmm.

YEAR	TEAM	LVL	AGE	WHIP	ERA	DRA	WARP	MPH	FB%	WHF	CSP
2017	NYA	MLB	29	0.87	2.35	3.01	1.4	94.3	38.9	10.7	42.5
2018	NYA	MLB	30	1.27	2.70	3.27	0.6	93.5	39	12	38.6
2018	SEA	MLB	30	1.38	3.74	5.44	-0.1	94.0	41.7	10.4	44.2
2019	SDN	MLB	31	1.40	5.34	5.02	0.1	93.2	30.8	10.3	39.7
2020	NYA	MLB	32	1.37	4.75	4.72	0.3	92.8	36.7	10.7	40.4

San Diego Padres 2020

Adam Warren, continued

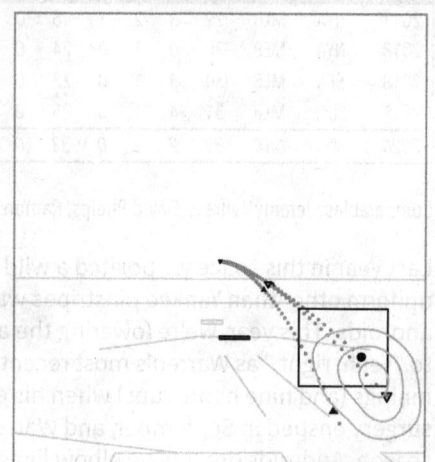

Pitch Shape vs LHH

Pitch Shape vs RHH

Type	Frequency	Velocity	H Movement	V Movement
● Fastball	30.6%	91.8 [98]	-3.4 [116]	-14.8 [103]
☐ Sinker				
+ Cutter				
▲ Changeup	17.8%	85.4 [101]	-13 [91]	-28.7 [96]
✕ Splitter				
▽ Slider	47.2%	86 [107]	5.6 [102]	-29 [112]
◇ Curveball	4.1%	79.2 [102]	8.1 [102]	-49.6 [96]
✥ Slow Curveball				
✱ Knuckleball				
▼ Screwball				

Trey Wingenter   RHP

Born: 04/15/94   Age: 26   Bats: R   Throws: R
Height: 6'7"   Weight: 200   Origin: Round 17, 2015 Draft (#507 overall)

YEAR	TEAM	LVL	AGE	W	L	SV	G	GS	IP	H	HR	BB/9	K/9	K	GB%	BABIP
2017	SAN	AA	23	2	1	20	49	0	47²	33	6	3.6	12.1	64	52%	.262
2018	ELP	AAA	24	3	3	4	40	0	44¹	29	4	4.9	10.8	53	48%	.250
2018	SDN	MLB	24	0	0	0	22	0	19	13	3	5.2	12.8	27	40%	.256
2019	SDN	MLB	25	1	3	1	51	1	51	34	5	4.9	12.7	72	37%	.269
2020	SDN	MLB	26	3	2	0	48	0	51	38	6	4.8	12.9	73	40%	.292

Comparables: Ryan Meisinger, Brad Boxberger, Ian Gibaut

Like the Padres as a whole, Wingenter flashed tremendous talent that never seemed to consistently produce strikes, outs and wins. As a young Padres reliever his high-90s heat is assured, and he abets it with a slider that flashes plus. But there's a lot of Wingenter to get moving in a coordinated fashion, and the young Alabaman can struggle with his mechanics and lose the plate. A few disasterpiece outings roughed up his overall numbers, but Wingenter's elite ability to miss bats will earn him plenty more chances to improve his command and become a late-inning leviathan.

YEAR	TEAM	LVL	AGE	WHIP	ERA	DRA	WARP	MPH	FB%	WHF	CSP
2017	SAN	AA	23	1.09	2.45	3.24	0.9				
2018	ELP	AAA	24	1.20	3.45	2.57	1.3				
2018	SDN	MLB	24	1.26	3.79	2.84	0.5	99.8	68.6	18.3	49.5
2019	SDN	MLB	25	1.22	5.65	3.55	1.0	98.1	55	16.7	45.2
2020	SDN	MLB	26	1.28	3.80	3.87	0.9	98.1	59.1	17.4	47.9

San Diego Padres 2020

Trey Wingenter, continued

Pitch Shape vs LHH

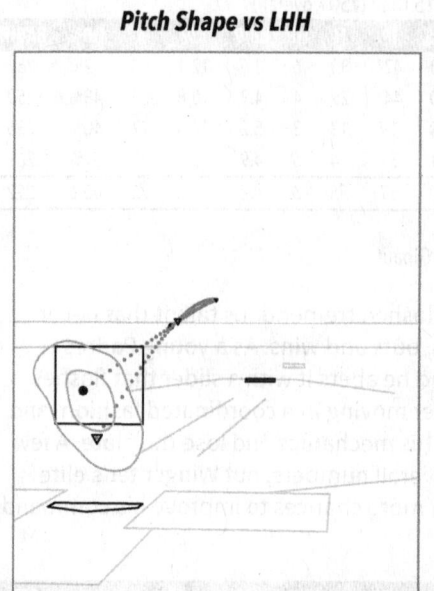

Pitch Shape vs RHH

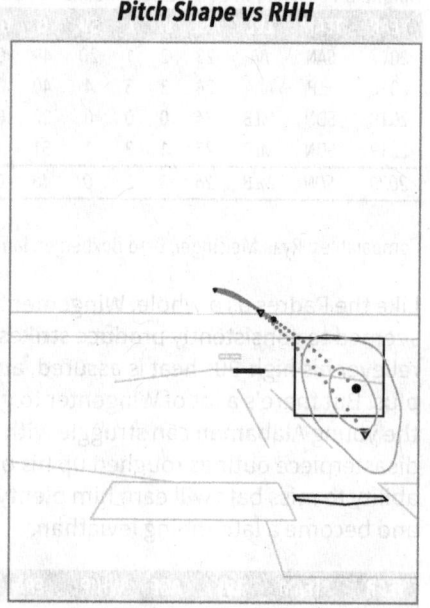

Type	Frequency	Velocity	H Movement	V Movement
● Fastball	55.0%	96.3 [111]	-7.8 [96]	-12.2 [110]
☐ Sinker				
+ Cutter				
▲ Changeup				
✕ Splitter				
▽ Slider	45.0%	86.1 [107]	2.2 [88]	-33.5 [99]
◇ Curveball				
⊕ Slow Curveball				
✳ Knuckleball				
▼ Screwball				

Kirby Yates   RHP
Born: 03/25/87   Age: 33   Bats: L   Throws: R
Height: 5'10"   Weight: 210   Origin: Round 26, 2005 Draft (#798 overall)

YEAR	TEAM	LVL	AGE	W	L	SV	G	GS	IP	H	HR	BB/9	K/9	K	GB%	BABIP
2017	SLC	AAA	30	0	0	1	6	0	7	8	0	3.9	18.0	14	60%	.533
2017	LAA	MLB	30	0	0	0	1	0	1	2	2	0.0	9.0	1	0%	.000
2017	SDN	MLB	30	4	5	1	61	0	55^2	42	10	3.1	14.1	87	30%	.296
2018	SDN	MLB	31	5	3	12	65	0	63	41	6	2.4	12.9	90	43%	.263
2019	SDN	MLB	32	0	5	41	60	0	60^2	41	2	1.9	15.0	101	48%	.325
2020	SDN	MLB	33	3	3	35	60	0	64	46	8	3.0	13.2	94	44%	.288

Comparables: Kevin Whelan, Zac Rosscup, Brandon Gomes

Ever since Bruce Sutter made the best hitters in the world look like they were swinging at an invisible feather, the splitter has been the most visually apt expression of a closer's dominance. Yates is the current split master, riding his tumbling terror to his first All-Star game last year and pacing the senior circuit in saves. The Kauai native upped his strikeout rate, cut his already low walk rate and kept the ball in the yard better than ever, leading to one of the top reliever seasons in baseball history by FIP and DRA. In a San Diego bullpen bursting with flame-throwing tyros, it's satisfying that the top dog is an undrafted, twice-sold, twice-released journeyman with a low-90s fastball who found success in his 30s with great command and a newfound pitch.

YEAR	TEAM	LVL	AGE	WHIP	ERA	DRA	WARP	MPH	FB%	WHF	CSP
2017	SLC	AAA	30	1.57	2.57	2.07	0.2				
2017	LAA	MLB	30	2.00	18.00	9.07	0.0	95.3	50	12.5	53.8
2017	SDN	MLB	30	1.10	3.72	3.10	1.3	95.6	62.9	18.8	48.3
2018	SDN	MLB	31	0.92	2.14	1.92	2.2	95.8	58.3	18.6	43.2
2019	SDN	MLB	32	0.89	1.19	2.03	2.2	94.8	57.1	17.1	44.4
2020	SDN	MLB	33	1.05	2.80	3.05	1.6	94.3	58.1	17.8	44.4

San Diego Padres 2020

Kirby Yates, continued

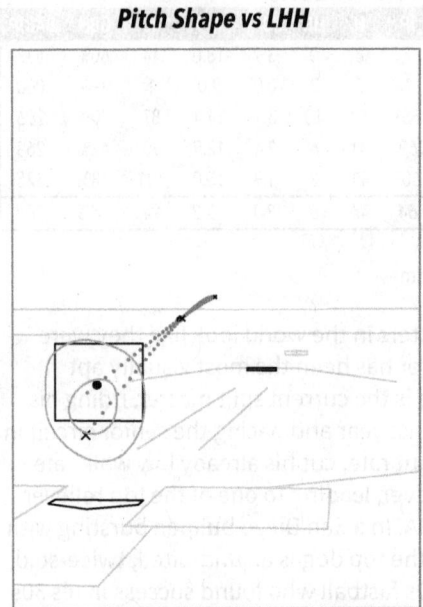
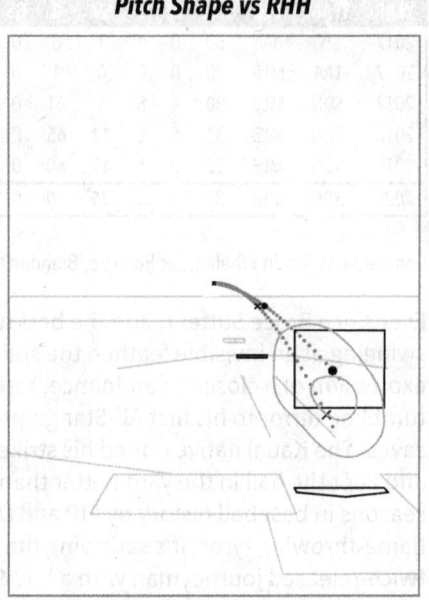

Pitch Shape vs LHH   *Pitch Shape vs RHH*

Type	Frequency	Velocity	H Movement	V Movement
● Fastball	57.1%	93.7 [104]	-11.7 [78]	-14.9 [103]
□ Sinker				
+ Cutter				
▲ Changeup				
✕ Splitter	42.0%	86.6 [106]	-11.1 [88]	-32.3 [90]
▽ Slider				
◇ Curveball				
✥ Slow Curveball				
✳ Knuckleball				
▼ Screwball				

PLAYER COMMENTS WITHOUT GRAPHS

CJ Abrams SS
Born: 10/03/00   Age: 19   Bats: L   Throws: R
Height: 6'2"   Weight: 185   Origin: Round 1, 2019 Draft (#6 overall)

YEAR	TEAM	LVL	AGE	PA	R	2B	3B	HR	RBI	BB	K	SB	CS	AVG/OBP/SLG
2019	PDR	RK	18	156	40	12	8	3	22	10	14	14	6	.401/.442/.662
2020	SDN	MLB	19	251	22	13	2	4	23	17	46	3	1	.240/.297/.360

Comparables: J.P. Crawford, Juan Soto, Justin Williams

The Padres' top pick in last summer's draft, Abrams burst onto the scene faster than a Hollywood studio green-lighting yet another uninspired sci-fi franchise reboot. The Georgia prep product has the type of raw speed that can warp space-time and a smooth lefty stroke that produces hit after hit, helping him bat over .400 en route to MVP honors in his rookie league debut. Abrams leverages his quick-twitch athleticism in the field and doesn't look lost at shortstop, but scouts worry that his funky throwing mechanics may precipitate a move to the keystone or center field, where his bat will more than play. His stroke is geared more for gappers than bombs so home run titles are an impossible mission, but Abrams makes consistent hard contact and there's a chance he could grow into at least league-average power while competing for batting and stolen base crowns. Coming soon to a ballpark near you.

YEAR	TEAM	LVL	AGE	PA	DRC+	VORP	BABIP	BRR	FRAA	WARP
2019	PDR	RK	18	156	199	24.1	.425	-0.7	SS(28): 6.9	2.5
2020	SDN	MLB	19	251	77	0.5	.286	0.0	SS 2	0.2

San Diego Padres 2020

Luis Campusano C

Born: 09/29/98 Age: 21 Bats: R Throws: R
Height: 5'10" Weight: 215 Origin: Round 2, 2017 Draft (#39 overall)

YEAR	TEAM	LVL	AGE	PA	R	2B	3B	HR	RBI	BB	K	SB	CS	AVG/OBP/SLG
2017	PDR	RK	18	98	3	4	0	1	13	6	14	0	1	.278/.327/.356
2017	SDP	RK	18	53	5	0	0	3	12	9	11	0	1	.250/.377/.455
2018	FTW	A	19	284	26	11	0	3	40	19	43	0	1	.288/.345/.365
2019	LEL	A+	20	487	63	31	1	15	81	52	57	0	0	.325/.396/.509
2020	SDN	MLB	21	251	26	12	0	7	28	17	46	0	0	.255/.310/.400

Comparables: Chance Sisco, Christian Vázquez, Gorkys Hernández

For a catcher, Campusano carries a big stick—literally, as he often used a 40-ounce cudgel to whack horsehides around the yard while winning the California League batting title and co-MVP honors last summer. He has all the tools you would want in a catching prospect: plus athleticism, agility behind the plate, solid receiving skills and a strong, accurate arm to go along with a disciplined batting eye and obvious power potential. Dude even idolizes Salvy Pérez. Campusano isn't quite a unicorn, but two-way backstops with plus tools are harder to find than Shiny Magikarp and the Padres may have been lucky enough to catch one.

YEAR	TEAM	LVL	AGE	PA	DRC+	VORP	BABIP	BRR	FRAA	WARP
2017	PDR	RK	18	98	110	0.0	.316	-1.7	C(17): -0.3	0.3
2017	SDP	RK	18	53	110	5.0	.267	0.3	C(10): -0.3	0.4
2018	FTW	A	19	284	118	6.1	.335	-1.1	C(38): -0.8, 1B(4): 0.2	1.2
2019	LEL	A+	20	487	168	44.6	.340	-4.4	C(76): -2.6, 1B(2): 0.0	3.9
2020	SDN	MLB	21	251	88	3.8	.292	-0.5	C 0, 1B 0	0.4

Franchy Cordero CF

Born: 09/02/94 Age: 25 Bats: L Throws: R
Height: 6'3" Weight: 175 Origin: International Free Agent, 2011

YEAR	TEAM	LVL	AGE	PA	R	2B	3B	HR	RBI	BB	K	SB	CS	AVG/OBP/SLG
2017	ELP	AAA	22	419	68	21	18	17	64	23	118	15	4	.326/.369/.603
2017	SDN	MLB	22	99	15	3	3	3	9	6	44	1	1	.228/.276/.424
2018	ELP	AAA	23	31	3	1	0	1	1	4	10	3	0	.259/.355/.407
2018	SDN	MLB	23	154	19	5	1	7	19	14	55	5	2	.237/.307/.439
2019	ELP	AAA	24	51	7	2	1	3	8	4	19	0	0	.217/.294/.500
2019	SDN	MLB	24	20	2	1	0	0	1	4	7	1	0	.333/.450/.400
2020	SDN	MLB	25	287	28	12	3	8	31	19	112	7	3	.227/.285/.386

Comparables: Byron Buxton, Wil Myers, Clint Frazier

"You could have all the talent in the world, but if you don't do the right thing, then nothing happens." DeNiro's bus-driving father character in *A Bronx Tale* could have been talking about Cordero, assuming you translate "the right thing" to mean focusing on defensive fundamentals and making more contact to help channel peerless natural athleticism, power and double-plus speed into consistent production. The only thing consistent in Franchy's game has been its inconsistency at the plate and in the field, and now that he's spent much of the last two seasons dealing with recurring elbow problems, we've seen a whole lot of "nothing happens" lately. Guys that whiff in over a third of their plate appearances rarely put it all together over the long haul, but a healthy Cordero could still tease out a .280/.330/.500 line in some future peak season and then draw years of paychecks from teams waiting in vain for him to repeat it.

YEAR	TEAM	LVL	AGE	PA	DRC+	VORP	BABIP	BRR	FRAA	WARP
2017	ELP	AAA	22	419	115	38.5	.431	1.7	CF(61): -2.5, LF(22): 1.5	2.2
2017	SDN	MLB	22	99	54	3.8	.400	1.2	CF(25): 0.8, LF(1): -0.1	0.0
2018	ELP	AAA	23	31	70	0.7	.375	0.6	CF(3): -0.8, LF(3): -0.4	-0.1
2018	SDN	MLB	23	154	72	4.7	.338	0.6	LF(22): 0.4, CF(11): -1.3	-0.2
2019	ELP	AAA	24	51	60	0.7	.292	0.5	CF(9): 0.6	0.0
2019	SDN	MLB	24	20	75	0.0	.556	0.6	CF(5): -0.4, RF(4): -0.3	0.0
2020	SDN	MLB	25	287	80	3.2	.362	1.0	CF -3, RF 0	0.0

Seth Mejias-Brean 3B

Born: 04/05/91 Age: 29 Bats: R Throws: R
Height: 6'2" Weight: 216 Origin: Round 8, 2012 Draft (#262 overall)

YEAR	TEAM	LVL	AGE	PA	R	2B	3B	HR	RBI	BB	K	SB	CS	AVG/OBP/SLG
2017	ARK	AA	26	323	31	8	2	3	42	22	71	4	1	.268/.328/.340
2017	LOU	AAA	26	66	6	1	0	0	1	3	9	0	1	.262/.318/.279
2017	TAC	AAA	26	77	15	6	1	1	7	7	13	1	0	.271/.338/.429
2018	ARK	AA	27	138	13	5	1	2	12	11	28	1	1	.238/.304/.341
2018	TAC	AAA	27	400	45	13	3	8	44	42	67	4	2	.266/.348/.389
2019	ELP	AAA	28	448	69	18	3	11	66	33	79	4	2	.316/.371/.455
2019	SDN	MLB	28	33	3	2	0	2	5	3	9	0	0	.233/.303/.500
2020	SDN	MLB	29	251	24	11	1	5	25	18	63	1	1	.244/.305/.367

Comparables: Travis Metcalf, Lane Adams, Chase d'Arnaud

"I just felt like I was floating. Running really fast, didn't know what happened. Just running the bases I was speechless. It was a dream come true." - *Seth Mejias-Brean, describing his first major-league home run*

Baseball is entertainment, joyful and beguiling. Major League Baseball is a business, cold and calculating. Time is a river, flowing and changing. They intertwine, shaping and coloring each other, and sometimes they conspire to bring us Mejias-Brean and his September call-up. The "career minor leaguer," as players who first reach the bigs in their late 20s are often called, acquitted himself well in San Diego, showing consistency at the plate and utility in the field. The odds are against Mejias-Brean and his .716 career Triple-A OPS ever gracing a major-league diamond again, but as fans we were happy to see and hear from him. When Fernando Tatís Jr. hit his first home run, it felt like destiny being fulfilled; when Mejias-Brean hit his, it felt like a wish being granted.

September rosters are slated to be reduced from 40 to 28 this year. Games will be faster, eyeballs and television remotes will have less chance to wander, and there will be fewer chances for players like Mejias-Brean to have their moment. The river gives, and the river takes away.

YEAR	TEAM	LVL	AGE	PA	DRC+	VORP	BABIP	BRR	FRAA	WARP
2017	ARK	AA	26	323	100	8.3	.339	-2.0	3B(69): -1.2, 1B(4): -0.4	0.7
2017	LOU	AAA	26	66	89	-3.3	.308	-0.1	1B(11): 0.8, 3B(4): 1.6	0.3
2017	TAC	AAA	26	77	91	3.0	.321	0.1	3B(19): 2.1	0.4
2018	ARK	AA	27	138	88	4.6	.292	0.5	3B(28): 2.9, 1B(4): -0.6	0.6
2018	TAC	AAA	27	400	94	16.2	.305	-0.9	3B(91): 6.5, 1B(6): -0.1	1.7
2019	ELP	AAA	28	448	93	15.9	.370	-3.0	3B(56): -5.3, SS(55): 4.2	1.1
2019	SDN	MLB	28	33	83	0.3	.263	0.2	1B(5): -0.1, SS(3): -0.1	0.0
2020	SDN	MLB	29	251	79	1.1	.314	-0.3	3B 2, SS 1	0.4

Luis Torrens C

Born: 05/02/96 Age: 24 Bats: R Throws: R
Height: 6'0" Weight: 175 Origin: International Free Agent, 2013

YEAR	TEAM	LVL	AGE	PA	R	2B	3B	HR	RBI	BB	K	SB	CS	AVG/OBP/SLG
2017	SDN	MLB	21	139	7	3	1	0	7	12	30	0	0	.163/.243/.203
2018	LEL	A+	22	515	62	36	3	6	73	26	77	1	1	.280/.320/.406
2019	AMA	AA	23	397	50	23	1	15	62	42	67	1	2	.300/.373/.500
2019	SDN	MLB	23	16	2	1	0	0	0	2	6	0	0	.214/.313/.286
2020	SDN	MLB	24	35	3	1	0	1	4	3	8	0	0	.223/.291/.351

Comparables: Del Crandall, Vic Janowicz, Raudy Read

Two full years removed from his sacrificial season on San Diego's 25-man roster, Torrens is back on prospect radars in DayGlo color after a breakthrough year in the Texas League. Torrens continues to be a rock behind the plate and has the defensive chops to be a big-league backup as soon as brunch tomorrow. The big news, though, is the noise his bat made during his Sod Poodle sojourn. Torrens suddenly added power to his already advanced approach and bat-to-ball skills, posting a .304/.373/.546 line and going deep 12 times after the All-Star break. He now has the look of a potential starting catcher, validating the Friars' Rule 5 gambit.

YEAR	TEAM	P. COUNT	FRM RUNS	BLK RUNS	THRW RUNS	TOT RUNS
2017	SDN	5274	-5.8	-2.5	0.0	-8.6
2019	AMA	12334	-2.8	0.0	5.2	2.2
2019	SDN	495	-0.1	0.4	0.0	1.0
2020	SDN	1331	-1.4	-0.2	0.2	-1.4

YEAR	TEAM	LVL	AGE	PA	DRC+	VORP	BABIP	BRR	FRAA	WARP
2017	SDN	MLB	21	139	61	-6.3	.215	1.1	C(51): -9.0	-0.8
2018	LEL	A+	22	515	100	26.2	.318	1.8	C(85): 1.0, 1B(3): 0.0	2.2
2019	AMA	AA	23	397	135	27.2	.331	-2.6	C(84): 3.0, 1B(1): 0.2	3.1
2019	SDN	MLB	23	16	75	0.2	.375	0.4	C(4): 0.4	0.1
2020	SDN	MLB	24	35	74	0.4	.272	-0.1	C -1	-0.1

Taylor Trammell OF

Born: 09/13/97 Age: 22 Bats: L Throws: L
Height: 6'2" Weight: 215 Origin: Round 1, 2016 Draft (#35 overall)

YEAR	TEAM	LVL	AGE	PA	R	2B	3B	HR	RBI	BB	K	SB	CS	AVG/OBP/SLG
2017	DYT	A	19	571	80	24	10	13	77	71	123	41	12	.281/.368/.450
2018	DAY	A+	20	461	71	19	4	8	41	58	105	25	10	.277/.375/.406
2019	CHT	AA	21	381	47	8	3	6	33	54	86	17	4	.236/.349/.336
2019	AMA	AA	21	133	14	4	1	4	10	13	36	3	4	.229/.316/.381
2020	SDN	MLB	22	35	4	1	0	1	4	3	10	1	0	.226/.305/.364

Comparables: Jesse Winker, Clint Frazier, Trent Grisham

The Padres are hoping the Franmil Reyes Trade, much like what was once called the James Shields Trade, will someday be called the Taylor Trammell trade. The former Reds farmhand boasts paint-peeling speed, power potential and the plus makeup needed to translate his tools into everyday production. Last year in Double-A, Trammell focused on drawing more walks with fewer strikeouts, but his more contact-oriented approach cost him much of his power. This year's focus should be on maintaining an advanced approach and getting on base while working to unleash the power in his swing. Trammell will need to improve his arm and his defensive fundamentals to stay in center, but his speed and on-base skills give him a fourth outfielder's floor with a much higher ceiling.

YEAR	TEAM	LVL	AGE	PA	DRC+	VORP	BABIP	BRR	FRAA	WARP
2017	DYT	A	19	571	127	43.1	.345	3.1	LF(104): -3.7, CF(17): -0.9	2.8
2018	DAY	A+	20	461	128	26.4	.358	-0.8	CF(60): -1.7, LF(29): 4.5	2.6
2019	CHT	AA	21	381	110	11.6	.299	2.1	LF(91): -0.7, CF(1): 0.1	1.5
2019	AMA	AA	21	133	89	-0.9	.295	-0.6	CF(30): -1.4	0.1
2020	SDN	MLB	22	35	84	0.6	.307	0.0	CF 0	0.1

Lake Bachar   RHP

Born: 06/03/95   Age: 25   Bats: R   Throws: R
Height: 6'3"   Weight: 215   Origin: Round 5, 2016 Draft (#144 overall)

YEAR	TEAM	LVL	AGE	W	L	SV	G	GS	IP	H	HR	BB/9	K/9	K	GB%	BABIP
2017	PDR	RK	22	1	0	0	5	0	9	5	1	6.0	15.0	15	44%	.235
2017	FTW	A	22	4	1	0	7	6	37^2	33	6	1.4	6.7	28	43%	.252
2018	LEL	A+	23	2	2	1	7	4	28^1	16	3	2.9	5.7	18	39%	.169
2018	SAN	AA	23	3	7	1	20	14	87	99	15	3.9	6.4	62	33%	.315
2019	LEL	A+	24	0	0	0	1	1	6	6	0	3.0	10.5	7	62%	.375
2019	AMA	AA	24	8	4	0	24	19	126^2	121	18	4.1	9.0	126	39%	.314
2020	SDN	MLB	25	2	2	0	33	0	35	36	7	3.3	7.5	29	37%	.292

Comparables: Drew Gagnon, Mario Hollands, Luis Santos

Bachar, once the punter and kicker for D-3 juggernaut Wisconsin-Whitewater's back-to-back NCAA championship squads, struck out more than a man per inning in the Amarillo rotation—an impressive feat given the obvious distraction of his father's cancer fight that prompted the Sod Poodles to hold a "Bachar Strong" fundraising promotion last August. He's not so much a prospect as a useful reminder that minor leaguers aren't tools and outcomes, but young men with lives, families, hopes and fears.

YEAR	TEAM	LVL	AGE	WHIP	ERA	DRA	WARP	MPH	FB%	WHF	CSP
2017	PDR	RK	22	1.22	1.00	3.43	0.2				
2017	FTW	A	22	1.04	4.06	3.67	0.7				
2018	LEL	A+	23	0.88	1.91	2.64	0.9				
2018	SAN	AA	23	1.57	5.59	6.70	-1.5				
2019	LEL	A+	24	1.33	3.00	5.48	0.0				
2019	AMA	AA	24	1.41	3.98	5.03	-0.2				
2020	SDN	MLB	25	1.41	5.15	5.14	0.1				

José Castillo   LHP

Born: 01/10/96   Age: 24   Bats: L   Throws: L
Height: 6'5"   Weight: 246   Origin: International Free Agent, 2012

YEAR	TEAM	LVL	AGE	W	L	SV	G	GS	IP	H	HR	BB/9	K/9	K	GB%	BABIP
2017	LEL	A+	21	3	2	1	39	0	47	38	0	4.2	9.4	49	42%	.297
2017	SAN	AA	21	1	0	0	8	0	9^1	8	1	3.9	9.6	10	28%	.292
2018	SAN	AA	22	2	1	5	12	0	15	14	0	4.8	15.6	26	38%	.438
2018	ELP	AAA	22	1	0	3	10	0	11^1	6	1	1.6	10.3	13	43%	.185
2018	SDN	MLB	22	3	3	0	37	0	38^1	23	3	2.8	12.2	52	39%	.250
2019	SDN	MLB	23	0	0	0	1	0	0^2	0	0	13.5	27.0	2	0%	.000
2020	SDN	MLB	24	2	1	0	30	0	32	24	3	5.0	9.9	35	37%	.269

Comparables: Mauricio Cabrera, Andrew Bellatti, Zack Littell

Castillo flashed nuclear stuff in his 2018 Padres debut, but cold, uncaring forces conspired to keep him off the mound last year. Forearm tightness in spring training limited him to infrequent minor-league rehab outings, a torn ligament in his hand ended his only Padres appearance and sanctions imposed by a very stable genius denied the lefty fireballer his annual Venezuelan Winter League stint. Castillo possesses a closer-level fastball/slider combo that can make big-league batsmen look silly, and if bad health doesn't intervene, he'll likely open another giant can of covfefe on them this summer.

YEAR	TEAM	LVL	AGE	WHIP	ERA	DRA	WARP	MPH	FB%	WHF	CSP
2017	LEL	A+	21	1.28	2.87	3.27	0.9				
2017	SAN	AA	21	1.29	2.89	4.36	0.0				
2018	SAN	AA	22	1.47	3.00	4.35	0.1				
2018	ELP	AAA	22	0.71	0.79	1.96	0.4				
2018	SDN	MLB	22	0.91	3.29	3.02	0.8	97.6	55.2	15.5	48.7
2019	SDN	MLB	23	1.50	0.00	5.18	0.0	96.7	64.7	11.8	37.4
2020	SDN	MLB	24	1.32	3.79	3.88	0.5	97.4	57.2	15.8	43.7

Miguel Díaz RHP

Born: 11/28/94 Age: 25 Bats: R Throws: R
Height: 6'0" Weight: 214 Origin: International Free Agent, 2011

YEAR	TEAM	LVL	AGE	W	L	SV	G	GS	IP	H	HR	BB/9	K/9	K	GB%	BABIP
2017	LEL	A+	22	0	0	0	2	2	7^1	8	0	3.7	6.1	5	44%	.348
2017	SDN	MLB	22	1	1	0	31	3	41^2	44	11	5.4	7.1	33	41%	.275
2018	SAN	AA	23	5	2	2	19	9	65	45	4	4.2	9.1	66	57%	.253
2018	ELP	AAA	23	0	3	0	5	2	13^1	17	2	8.8	10.1	15	40%	.375
2018	SDN	MLB	23	1	0	0	11	0	18^2	16	2	5.8	14.5	30	35%	.341
2019	AMA	AA	24	2	1	0	6	4	22^2	21	9	3.2	13.1	33	30%	.255
2019	ELP	AAA	24	0	1	0	4	4	7^2	8	1	2.3	8.2	7	38%	.350
2019	SDN	MLB	24	0	0	0	5	0	6^1	9	1	1.4	5.7	4	36%	.381
2020	SDN	MLB	25	2	2	0	33	0	35	38	9	4.1	10.0	39	38%	.317

Comparables: Jose Cisnero, Dean Deetz, Elieser Hernandez

Three years after coming to the Padres as a Rule 5 draftee, Díaz remains a stereotypical relief pitching prospect. Like so many others, his fastball can reach the mid-90s but he doesn't command it well. His breaking ball and changeup have their moments, but with little consistency. He can miss bats with regularity, but he also misses targets. Díaz is coming off a season plagued by recurring knee problems, but after sanding some of the rough edges off his delivery, he posted a much-improved walk rate during his short time in the high minors. That bodes well for his potential future as a stereotypical middle reliever.

YEAR	TEAM	LVL	AGE	WHIP	ERA	DRA	WARP	MPH	FB%	WHF	CSP
2017	LEL	A+	22	1.50	3.68	5.61	0.0				
2017	SDN	MLB	22	1.66	7.34	7.15	-0.9	98.2	65.5	9.3	47.1
2018	SAN	AA	23	1.15	2.35	2.78	1.8				
2018	ELP	AAA	23	2.25	8.10	7.36	-0.3				
2018	SDN	MLB	23	1.50	4.82	3.24	0.4	97.8	55.3	17.9	45.5
2019	AMA	AA	24	1.28	4.37	4.35	0.1				
2019	ELP	AAA	24	1.30	2.35	4.16	0.2				
2019	SDN	MLB	24	1.58	7.11	5.29	0.0	96.9	52.9	7.8	49
2020	SDN	MLB	25	1.55	6.23	6.12	-0.3	97.6	62.1	12.2	48.5

San Diego Padres 2020

MacKenzie Gore LHP
Born: 02/24/99   Age: 21   Bats: L   Throws: L
Height: 6'3"   Weight: 195   Origin: Round 1, 2017 Draft (#3 overall)

YEAR	TEAM	LVL	AGE	W	L	SV	G	GS	IP	H	HR	BB/9	K/9	K	GB%	BABIP
2017	PDR	RK	18	0	1	0	7	7	21^1	14	0	3.0	14.3	34	69%	.333
2018	FTW	A	19	2	5	0	16	16	60^2	61	5	2.7	11.0	74	41%	.354
2019	LEL	A+	20	7	1	0	15	15	79^1	36	4	2.3	12.5	110	38%	.211
2019	AMA	AA	20	2	1	0	5	5	21^2	20	3	3.3	10.4	25	40%	.308
2020	SDN	MLB	21	2	3	0	8	8	38	37	6	4.1	11.6	49	40%	.335

Comparables: Bryse Wilson, José Berríos, Henry Owens

Last summer's landmark case *Bush Leagues v. Gore, 1.02 ERA (2019)* ended in a unanimous ruling that the young left-hander is baseball's top pitching prospect. Gore laid waste to California League hitters with uncommon command of his lively mid-90s fastball, two quality breakers and a changeup that flashed plus. He's athletic, fluid, dynamic, poised, aggressive, confident, consistent, prepared, competitive, solidly built, blister-free and just barely old enough to order a Ballast Point Victory At Sea Imperial Porter. A few months building up his innings count and dominating more advanced Double-A hitters might be enough to land him in Petco, where a future at the front of the rotation awaits.

YEAR	TEAM	LVL	AGE	WHIP	ERA	DRA	WARP	MPH	FB%	WHF	CSP
2017	PDR	RK	18	0.98	1.27	0.48	1.3				
2018	FTW	A	19	1.30	4.45	4.11	0.8				
2019	LEL	A+	20	0.71	1.02	1.70	3.2				
2019	AMA	AA	20	1.29	4.15	4.20	0.2				
2020	SDN	MLB	21	1.43	4.83	4.91	0.4				

Javy Guerra RHP
Born: 09/25/95 Age: 24 Bats: L Throws: R
Height: 5'11" Weight: 155 Origin: International Free Agent, 2012

YEAR	TEAM	LVL	AGE	W	L	SV	G	GS	IP	H	HR	BB/9	K/9	K	GB%	BABIP
2019	LEL	A+	23	0	0	1	17	0	17	13	2	2.6	12.2	23	34%	.306
2019	SDN	MLB	23	0	0	0	8	0	8^2	7	3	3.1	6.2	6	48%	.167
2020	SDN	MLB	24	1	2	0	30	0	32	35	5	3.3	7.8	27	46%	.314

Comparables: Brandon Gomes, Drew Smith, Tony Gonsolin

Data Point #12,246 proving Baseball Is Cuh-RAY-Zee: Guerra, four years after being traded from Boston and four months after the former shortstop threw his first professional pitch, completed his September in the Padres 'pen with a better WARP than the superstar closer he was traded for, Craig Kimbrel. Sure, he was "better" only in the "not quite so far below replacement level" sense, but the fact Guerra showed enough in his minor-league debut to earn his call-up is a minor miracle. The young Panamanian's heavy fastball can reach triple-digits, his slider is workable and he can control them both surprisingly well. Improved command and pitchability are the next order of business, but Guerra has already proven to be a quick study, with all the tools needed to work high-leverage innings.

YEAR	TEAM	LVL	AGE	WHIP	ERA	DRA	WARP	MPH	FB%	WHF	CSP
2019	LEL	A+	23	1.06	3.71	3.67	0.2				
2019	SDN	MLB	23	1.15	5.19	6.10	-0.1	100.2	76.9	8.2	52.6
2020	SDN	MLB	24	1.47	5.36	5.45	0.0	100.0	79.2	8.5	54.2

Adrian Morejon   LHP

Born: 02/27/99   Age: 21   Bats: L   Throws: L
Height: 6'0"   Weight: 175   Origin: International Free Agent, 2016

YEAR	TEAM	LVL	AGE	W	L	SV	G	GS	IP	H	HR	BB/9	K/9	K	GB%	BABIP
2017	TRI	A-	18	2	2	0	7	7	35^1	37	2	0.8	8.9	35	41%	.337
2017	FTW	A	18	1	2	0	6	6	27^2	28	2	4.2	7.5	23	34%	.321
2018	LEL	A+	19	4	4	0	13	13	62^2	54	6	3.4	10.1	70	55%	.302
2019	AMA	AA	20	0	4	0	16	16	36	29	3	3.8	11.0	44	51%	.292
2019	SDN	MLB	20	0	0	0	5	2	8	15	1	3.4	10.1	9	37%	.483
2020	SDN	MLB	21	1	2	0	15	3	29	31	5	3.6	7.8	25	42%	.308

Comparables: Tyler Skaggs, Jenrry Mejia, Chris Tillman

Three years after signing with San Diego for $11 million, Morejon remains a top-flight starting prospect more in theory than practice. The young Cuban can unleash rare lefty heat that sits comfortably in the mid-90s and a changeup and curve which could both become quality offerings, but nagging injuries continue to limit his opportunities to polish them and fan the whispers that his frame won't hold up to a starter's workload. Morejon was knocked around during his brief July call-up, yet still tantalized with his swing-and-miss stuff. If Job One this year is proving he can take the ball every fifth day, Job Two is developing the command and consistency necessary for a big-league rotation spot.

YEAR	TEAM	LVL	AGE	WHIP	ERA	DRA	WARP	MPH	FB%	WHF	CSP
2017	TRI	A-	18	1.13	3.57	4.30	0.4				
2017	FTW	A	18	1.48	4.23	5.57	-0.1				
2018	LEL	A+	19	1.24	3.30	3.49	1.3				
2019	AMA	AA	20	1.22	4.25	2.75	1.0				
2019	SDN	MLB	20	2.25	10.12	5.09	0.0	97.9	53.9	9.7	50.7
2020	SDN	MLB	21	1.47	5.23	5.29	0.1	98.1	56.5	10.2	53.1

Luis Patiño RHP

Born: 10/26/99   Age: 20   Bats: R   Throws: R
Height: 6'0"   Weight: 192   Origin: International Free Agent, 2016

YEAR	TEAM	LVL	AGE	W	L	SV	G	GS	IP	H	HR	BB/9	K/9	K	GB%	BABIP
2017	DPA	RK	17	2	1	0	4	4	16	11	0	1.1	8.4	15	58%	.256
2017	PDR	RK	17	2	1	0	9	8	40	32	2	3.6	9.7	43	50%	.286
2018	FTW	A	18	6	3	0	17	17	83^1	65	1	2.6	10.6	98	45%	.320
2019	LEL	A+	19	6	8	0	18	17	87	61	4	3.5	11.7	113	40%	.278
2019	AMA	AA	19	0	0	0	2	2	7^2	8	0	4.7	11.7	10	19%	.381
2020	SDN	MLB	20	2	2	0	33	0	35	34	5	3.6	9.8	38	37%	.315

Comparables: Mike Soroka, Taijuan Walker, Jordan Lyles

The most impressive thing about Patiño's 2019 season wasn't how he breezed through the California League as a teenager; it was the way he matured throughout the year from thrower to pitcher. His darting slider misses bats, but his bread and butter is a lively high-90s fastball, which was enough to dominate lower leagues but couldn't stand on its own against more advanced hitters. As the year wore on, Patiño cut his walk rate, improved his command and worked on his changeup, which has grown into more than a show-me pitch. He'll be tested in Double-A this summer and has yet to shoulder a heavy innings load, but Patiño's raw stuff and improving pitchability gives him a Sistene ceiling.

YEAR	TEAM	LVL	AGE	WHIP	ERA	DRA	WARP	MPH	FB%	WHF	CSP
2017	DPA	RK	17	0.81	1.69	1.90	0.7				
2017	PDR	RK	17	1.20	2.47	2.60	1.5				
2018	FTW	A	18	1.07	2.16	2.87	2.3				
2019	LEL	A+	19	1.09	2.69	2.71	2.4				
2019	AMA	AA	19	1.57	1.17	4.52	0.0				
2020	SDN	MLB	20	1.37	4.45	4.49	0.4				

San Diego Padres 2020

LINEOUTS

Hitters

HITTER	POS	TEAM	LVL	AGE	PA	R	2B	3B	HR	RBI	BB	K	SB	CS	AVG/OBP/SLG	DRC+	WARP
Gabriel Arias	SS	LEL	A+	19	511	62	21	4	17	75	25	128	8	4	.302/.339/.470	122	2.1
Allen Cordoba	UT	LEL	A+	23	470	68	20	6	5	43	31	77	32	11	.301/.367/.412	127	4.0
Jake Cronenworth	UT	DUR	AAA	25	406	75	26	4	10	45	49	62	12	5	.334/.429/.520	138	3.4
Michael Gettys	CF	ELP	AAA	23	551	97	29	5	31	91	33	168	14	6	.256/.305/.517	79	1.0
Hudson Head	CF	PDR	Rk	18	141	19	7	3	1	12	15	29	3	3	.283/.383/.417	125	0.1
Tucupita Marcano	INF	FTW	A	19	504	55	19	3	2	45	35	45	15	16	.270/.323/.337	92	0.3
Owen Miller	INF	AMA	AA	22	560	76	28	2	13	68	46	86	5	5	.290/.355/.430	112	3.4
Edward Olivares	OF	AMA	AA	23	551	85	25	2	18	77	43	98	35	10	.283/.349/.453	114	2.9
Jorge Ona	LF	AMA	AA	22	103	11	2	0	5	18	11	26	2	1	.348/.417/.539	170	0.6
Tirso Ornelas	RF	LEL	A+	19	379	41	11	5	1	30	44	91	3	1	.220/.309/.292	67	-0.9
	RF	PDR	Rk	19	97	6	2	0	0	11	9	22	4	0	.205/.278/.227	51	-0.2
Hudson Potts	INF	AMA	AA	20	448	56	23	1	16	59	32	128	3	1	.227/.290/.406	58	-1.2
Boog Powell	CF	ELP	AAA	26	403	66	25	1	8	37	59	94	14	0	.288/.391/.438	94	1.0
Esteban Quiroz	2B	ELP	AAA	27	366	64	25	0	19	66	52	82	3	1	.271/.384/.539	120	2.0
Buddy Reed	OF	AMA	AA	24	441	49	15	2	14	50	42	126	23	8	.228/.310/.388	84	2.0
Jeisson Rosario	CF	LEL	A+	19	525	67	14	4	3	35	87	114	11	4	.242/.372/.314	118	3.3
Esteury Ruiz	2B	LEL	A+	20	380	45	18	2	6	36	26	101	34	11	.239/.300/.357	71	-0.5

Last season's addition of power to his already superlative glove and cannon arm gives Venezuelan teenager **Gabriel Arias** a first-division shortstop's ceiling, but his free-swinging ways will likely keep him from reaching it. ⚾ Former Rule 5 martyr **Allen Córdoba** recovered from injury and a season's worth of big-league PTSD to post a bounce-back year in High-A; having moved from shortstop to left field while flashing speed and contact skills, his ceiling is late-career Lonnie Smith without the walks. ⚾ One of a new breed of "utility pitchers," **Jake Cronenworth** was the minor league player of the year for the Durham Bulls. ⚾ **Michael Gettys** has speed, plus range in center, a rifle arm and a newly-minted El Paso home run record; he may be the most powerful Chihuahua in history, but his career-long propensity to chase strike three makes it unlikely he'll spend much time playing with the big dogs. ⚾ Ambidextrous high school quarterback **Hudson Head** used both hands to dig into his $3 million bonus (a third-round record) while flashing speed, a strong arm, power potential and a surprisingly mature approach in his Rookie League debut; he has all the tools you look for in an All-Star center fielder. ⚾ Like most teenagers, **Tucupita Marcano** couldn't wait to get out of Fort Wayne and move to the coast, taking his high-contact speed game to Lake Elsinore for the High-A playoffs. He likely won't hit for power, but natural bat-to-ball skills and a high baseball IQ could earn him a utility infield spot some day. ⚾ From Ozaukee to Normal to Amarillo, **Owen Miller** has hit every place they bother to chalk lines, is a solid defender and held his own during an aggressive full-season debut in Double-A; his arm is stretched at shortstop and his line-drive stroke isn't geared for power, but the young Sconnie fits the profile of a bat-first second sacker. ⚾ **Edward Olivares** passed his Double-A weeder course last summer while setting career highs in batting average, OBP, home runs and steals. He's not a plus center fielder but has the arm for right and his power/speed combo will work well as a fourth outfielder. ⚾ Despite a season cut short by shoulder surgery, **Jorge Oña** hit so well it made watching Jorge Oña play defense seem palatable. Given the depth of the system and the roughness of his edges, the Padres gambled a bit when they added him to the 40-man, but the upside is sizable. ⚾ It's all about the projection for **Tirso Ornelas**, who cratered in his first full professional season but made strides at the plate after reworking his swing. The Tijuana native possesses the mature approach, athleticism, power potential and makeup to grow into a productive right fielder. ⚾ Former first-round pick **Hudson Potts** spent last summer too young to order a Shiner Bock in Amarillo, where he struggled to make contact but improved as the season wore on; a return Double-A engagement should help sort out whether his prospect buzz has gone flat or heady days as a hot corner power bat are in his future. ⚾ After cracking eight home runs in El Paso's launching pad last summer Boog The Younger is now only 371 dingers away from becoming the most powerful **Boog Powell** in the history of professional baseball. Then again, gentle reader, you yourself are only 399 away. ⚾ The sheer volume of 2019 PCL breakouts makes it difficult to sort the true-talent wheat from the ball-boosted chaff, but **Esteban Quiroz** has a good case to be considered among the former: namely, a knack for getting on base nearly 40 percent of the time. The time is ripe for the 28-year-old to see at least a grain of major-league experience in 2020. ⚾ His name may sound like he played drums with Charlie Parker, but **Buddy Reed** is actually a switch-hitting center fielder with elite speed and athleticism whose inability to find any consistent rhythm in the batter's box will likely keep him from bebopping his way to The Show. ⚾ Sure, signing a five-tool 16-year-old wunderkind like **Emmanuel Rodriguez** for $2.5 million is cool, but have you tried turning one of those guys into a productive big-leaguer in less than six years? ⚾ **Jeisson Rosario** showed off plus defensive chops in the center pasture and a surprisingly patient approach for a teenager in High-A, though he struggled to make consistent contact. The tools are here for him to grow into the top-of-the-order lefty pest every team craves. ⚾ Even in a Padres organization overstuffed with premium talent, **Esteury Ruiz** is notable for his speed and raw athleticism, but the young Dominican has shown a propensity to chase, struggles to make consistent contact and is a poor defender at the keystone; he's still only 21, but a slide down the defensive spectrum will make it even less likely his bat will play.

San Diego Padres 2020

Pitchers

PITCHER	TEAM	LVL	AGE	W	L	SV	G	GS	IP	H	HR	BB/9	K/9	K	GB%	WHIP	ERA	DRA	WARP
Pedro Avila	PDR	Rk	22	0	1	0	3	2	10	5	0	1.8	13.5	15	40%	0.70	0.90	1.91	0.4
	AMA	AA	22	0	2	0	3	3	12	14	4	4.5	9.8	13	33%	1.67	8.25	6.37	-0.2
	SDN	MLB	22	0	0	0	1	1	5^1	4	0	3.4	8.4	5	40%	1.12	1.69	4.41	0.1
David Bednar	AMA	AA	24	2	5	14	44	0	58	49	4	2.8	13.3	86	50%	1.16	2.95	3.36	0.9
	SDN	MLB	24	0	2	0	13	0	11	10	3	4.1	11.5	14	34%	1.36	6.55	4.50	0.1
Ronald Bolanos	LEL	A+	22	5	2	0	10	10	53^2	37	4	3.9	9.1	54	50%	1.12	2.85	3.37	1.1
	AMA	AA	22	8	5	0	15	13	76^2	71	7	3.5	10.3	88	48%	1.32	4.23	4.88	0.0
	SDN	MLB	22	0	2	0	5	3	19^2	17	3	5.5	8.7	19	41%	1.47	5.95	6.03	-0.1
Joey Cantillo	FTW	A	19	9	3	0	19	19	98	58	3	2.5	11.8	128	46%	0.87	1.93	2.18	3.5
	LEL	A+	19	1	1	0	3	3	13^2	12	2	4.6	10.5	16	38%	1.39	4.61	3.75	0.2
Henry Henry	FTW	A	20	7	5	10	43	0	81^1	73	3	1.8	8.9	80	50%	1.09	3.32	3.64	1.1
Reggie Lawson	AMA	AA	21	3	1	0	6	6	27^2	28	4	4.2	11.7	36	39%	1.48	5.20	4.99	0.0
Aaron Loup	SDN	MLB	31	0	0	0	4	0	3^1	2	0	2.7	13.5	5	57%	0.90	0.00	4.43	0.0
Jacob Nix	LEL	A+	23	0	2	0	2	2	8^2	10	1	3.1	11.4	11	63%	1.50	3.12	3.90	0.1
	ELP	AAA	23	1	0	0	2	2	11	7	1	0.8	9.8	12	42%	0.73	0.82	2.22	0.5
Franklin Van Gurp	AUG	A	23	2	0	4	16	0	28^2	21	4	2.8	12.6	40	45%	1.05	3.77	3.34	0.5
	FTW	A	23	0	1	1	9	0	15^2	16	0	2.9	9.2	16	49%	1.34	2.87	4.47	0.1
	LEL	A+	23	1	3	0	14	0	18^1	26	0	7.4	9.3	19	40%	2.24	6.38	10.25	-1.2
Ryan Weathers	FTW	A	19	3	7	0	22	22	96	101	6	1.7	8.4	90	46%	1.24	3.84	5.46	-0.3
Jimmy Yacabonis	NOR	AAA	27	2	2	2	17	0	24	26	2	5.6	8.2	22	51%	1.71	4.50	6.07	0.0
	BAL	MLB	27	1	2	0	29	4	41	51	9	5.3	7.2	33	36%	1.83	6.80	8.17	-1.2

Over a 10-day span in April **Pedro Avila** experienced both the zenith and nadir of baseball prospectdom, baffling the Diamondbacks over five-plus innings in a triumphant debut before hurting his elbow in his next Texas League start; he'll spend 2020 recovering from last fall's Tommy John surgery. ⓫ Former 35th-round pick **David Bednar** has ridden a mid-90s fastball, a functional curve and a splitter he learned from Hideo Nomo all the way from Lafayette University to the San Diego 'pen; there's enough swing-and-miss here to envision a solid career in middle relief. ⓫ Live-armed Cuban **Ronald Bolaños** rode his mid-90s heat all the way from High-A to San Diego last year, but spotty control, indifferent secondaries and inconsistent mechanics may well send him to the bullpen. ⓫ A rare Padres pitching prospect who doesn't light up radar guns, **Joey Cantillo** dominated the Midwest League as a teenager with advanced pitchability and tremendous feel for his plus changeup; if the same tricks work this year against more advanced hitters he'll vault up prospect lists. ⓫ Another year, another setback for former top prospect **Anderson Espinoza**, as he underwent his second Tommy John procedure last April. ⓫ The Padres moved **Henry Henry** to the Fort Wayne bullpen last year, with encouraging results; his fastball/slider mix may not match the high octane stuff of so many other San Diego relief prospects, but he probably has a leg up on repeating his delivery. ⚾ **Brett Kennedy** wasn't particularly good for the Padres in 2018 and isn't particularly healthy now, as spring training arm fatigue that morphed into a bum shoulder kept him on the shelf all last season. ⚾ Long, lean **Reggie Lawson** only made six starts in Amarillo before experiencing elbow pain; he avoided surgery and resurfaced in the Arizona Fall League, where his mid-90s fastball and potentially plus curve delivered reasonable impersonations of big-league offerings. ⚾ Lefty sidearmer **Aaron Loup**'s first foray into free agency featured $1.4 million earned and 14 batters faced before his second elbow injury in as many years landed him on the shelf. ⚾ "There is only one thing in life worse than being talked about, and that is not being talked about," said Oscar Wilde. "Unless you're a fringy young starter in a loaded organization who just sat out a full year with a sore elbow and is making headlines after getting wasted, and allegedly trying to enter a stranger's house through the doggy door and getting yourself kicked, tased and arrested," added **Jacob Nix**. ⚾ **Franklin Van Gurp**, of the Saint Maarten Van Gurps, has completed his schooling at Chipola and Florida International and is pursuing a career in the entertainment industry. After his involvement in last June's Alex Dickerson trade, he summered in Lake Elsinore and Fort Wayne, where he spent his days tossing sinkers and sliders and handing out way too many free passes. ⚾ Top 2018 pick **Ryan Weathers** got off to a great start in his full-season debut before losing a month to a forearm issue and struggling through diminished velocity the rest of the way. ⚾ The twelfth time someone gets optioned, no matter how many different roles they've pitched in or how good their arm is, it can be considered the cost of doing business. But **Jimmy Yacabonis** was optioned a thirteenth time in August and the Orioles finally had enough, banishing him to Triple-A.

Padres Prospects

The State of the System
It's almost unfair that the Padres system could graduate two rookie-of-the-year candidates and still be this good.

The Top Ten

★ ★ ★ *2020 Top 101 Prospect* **#5** ★ ★ ★

1
MacKenzie Gore   LHP   OFP: 70   ETA: 2020
Born: 02/24/99   Age: 21   Bats: L   Throws: L   Height: 6'3"   Weight: 195
Origin: Round 1, 2017 Draft (#3 overall)

The Report: There's not much we can say here that we haven't said many times over this year. Gore will enter 2020 as the top pitching prospect in baseball after thoroughly decimating the hitter-friendly California League last season before dipping his 20-year-old toes in Double-A water in the second half. Blisters derailed his 2018 season and limited him to 60 innings, so the club took a mindful approach to his workload, limiting him to just five appearances and 20ish innings after his July 2nd promotion to park him smooth and tidy at 100 for the year, with a presumable eye towards tacking on another 40 or so again next year. I wrote at mid-season that Gore made just about the strongest case an A-ball pitcher could make to be considered the top prospect in all of baseball, and nothing about his abbreviated Double-A stint changed that at all.

It's four above-average-or-better pitches, highlighted by a fastball that'll work into the mid 90s with rare explosiveness and finish. His curve's a nasty yakker, he can land a tight slider below either side of the zone, and the change moves late with plus velocity separation. If you want to pick nits the control can wander around a little when the delivery disjoints, but, well, he's 20 and that happens.

Variance: Moderate; or, put another way, as low as it can get for a 20-year-old prep arm.

Mark Barry's Fantasy Take: Well it's no longer even a lukewarm take to peg Gore as the best pitching prospect in the game, but still, to reiterate, Gore is the best pitching prospect in the game. He's still a pitcher, though, which brings some risk, but his ceiling is top-10 starter in baseball. Me likey (are people still saying "me likey"? Were they ever? Nevermind, this isn't the place for that. Moving on).

2

★ ★ ★ *2020 Top 101 Prospect* **#15** ★ ★ ★

Luis Patiño   RHP   OFP: 70   ETA: 2021
Born: 10/26/99   Age: 20   Bats: R   Throws: R   Height: 6'0"   Weight: 192
Origin: International Free Agent, 2016

The Report: The entire package isn't quite as advanced, nor is the stuff quite as impressive, as Gore's. But which one has the higher upside is a legitimate conversation to have, and Patiño is eight months younger. That should tell you all you need to know about just how good this kid was this year, and could become in years future. As a right-hander who barely scrapes 6-feet, he's exactly the kind of archetype who would've been vulnerable to institutional biases and corresponding whispers of an inevitable bullpen future in days past, but there wasn't much of anything in his stuff, performance, or countenance this year that pointed even faintly in that direction. The delivery mirrors Gore's from the right side, with a similar high leg kick though with a more deliberate turn downhill, and while he lacks the lefty's elite athleticism he's got more than enough to hold the delivery together. There's some crossfire to it that'll wobble the command at times, but the deception he creates is a helpful cake-topper for what is on its own a nasty combination of pitches.

It's high-end stuff; as with Gore, there are four pitches here that present at least above-average, including three I hung 6s or better on at mid-season. A high three-quarters slot with the aforementioned crossfire creates a fun angle for him to impart horizontal action on his pitches, though he'll need to further refine his change and a developing cut look on his fastball to eat into some present split issues with left-handed hitters. There may be some ongoing control issues that crop up while he finishes growing into an adult body, but we're reasonably confident his physicality and extremely mature approach to his craft will be enough to overcome those concerns and that he'll develop enough command to allow for near-full utility of the impressive raw stuff.

Variance: Moderately High; or, put another way, pretty damn low for a kid who pitched his way to Double-A at 19.

Mark Barry's Fantasy Take: If you think it's unfair that the Padres can back up Gore with Patiño in their system, well, I agree. The righty answered any questions about his pop-up status by fanning 123 dudes in 94 2/3 innings, getting to Double-A as a 19-year-old. All of those things are good. While he finished at the same level as Gore, his age and volatility probably keep him from the immediate doorstep to the big league rotation, knocking him down a bit, but he's still a top-50 dynasty name for me.

3

★ ★ ★ *2020 Top 101 Prospect* **#33** ★ ★ ★

CJ Abrams   SS   OFP: 60   ETA: 2022
Born: 10/03/00   Age: 19   Bats: L   Throws: R   Height: 6'2"   Weight: 185
Origin: Round 1, 2019 Draft (#6 overall)

The Report: Fresh out of the draft, you'd expect someone with the skills of CJ Abrams taken in the top 10 to automatically rest atop his organization's rankings. Slotting Abrams third isn't an indictment of his ability, but speaks to the depth of the Padres system as it currently stands. A premium athlete playing a premium position, the upside potential is sky high. His quick movements in short bursts, along with speed in longer distances every bit as impressive, combine to give him range at shortstop. He's a top-of-the-scale runner who can take just a ton of extra bases. His first foray into pro ball at the complex level was impressive, and he emphatically answered some of the questions that rumbled prior to the draft about the thump he'd be able to generate. The swing is explosive, and he generates loud contact, though he'll leak to the front-side at present.

He'd be physically capable of playing pretty much anywhere, though he currently lacks for arm strength. He's still much thinner right now than he will be, and his frame will support a big transformation in the coming years that will challenge his balance between heavy strength or lean quickness. That leaves the biggest question to his ultimate potential resting on his hitting coaches and his desire to listen and make adjustments.

Variance: Very high. There are players all around the big leagues who hang their hat on running and playing defense. If he can grow offensively in keeping with his potential, he will be a top-of-the-order menace for years.

Mark Barry's Fantasy Take: We didn't see much of Abrams outside of the AZL, but what we did see was, uh, good. He just turned 19 years old, so he's still a little raw, but we're looking at a guy that could hit 15-20 homers and snag 30 bases while not killing you with the batting average. There's even upside for a little more if it all clicks.

★ ★ ★ *2020 Top 101 Prospect* **#67** ★ ★ ★

4 **Luis Campusano** C OFP: 60 ETA: 2021
Born: 09/29/98 Age: 21 Bats: R Throws: R Height: 5'10" Weight: 215
Origin: Round 2, 2017 Draft (#39 overall)

The Report: The Georgia high school product was the 39th-overall pick, and the first catcher selected in the 2017 draft. That kind of pedigree is rare air for a prep catcher, and Campusano responded last year by winning a batting title and sharing an MVP in the California League as a 20-year-old. The right-handed hitter was a doubles machine, swatting 31 of 'em while walking nearly as often as he struck out. Campusano's exceptional strike zone awareness and selectivity results in consistent, professional at-bats. He attacks pitches you want a hitter to attack and frequently finds barrel when he does. His gap-to-gap approach is really mature, and natural strength can produce plenty of extra-base hits.

Meanwhile, his athleticism and mobility provide a strong defensive foundation behind the plate. His blocking, receiving, and throwing abilities are all solid, although he'll need to further refine his catch-and-release to improve upon last season's inconsistent throwing game. He'll pop 1.8s and 1.9s, though, and he has the physical tools and arm strength to improve.

Campusano's leadership qualities and gritty competitiveness are evident when you watch him play. His advanced offensive ability is extremely valuable from the catcher position, and he could force DH or first base starts when getting a break from catching. Continued improvement of his defensive abilities could make Campusano a primary big league backstop. His floor may be the offensive side of a catching platoon.

Variance: Moderate; he's a prep catcher, and they take time and often random routes. But Campusano is an all-around, everyday catcher for a good baseball team with first-division upside.

Mark Barry's Fantasy Take: Sure, I could take the lazy way out and say "Dynasty catcher, no thanks lol", but a) I would never not give you my all and b) I actually really like Campusano. His patience and contact-oriented approach at the dish raise his floor, and his prowess behind said dish should satisfy the requisite defensive threshold. The only drawback on Campusano is that he's currently behind defensive wizard Austin Hedges and the enigmatic Francisco Mejia on the depth chart. As far as drawbacks go, that's not too bad, as these things tend to work themselves out.

───── ★ ★ ★ *2020 Top 101 Prospect* **#69** ★ ★ ★ ─────

5 **Taylor Trammell   OF**   OFP: 55   ETA: 2020/21
Born: 09/13/97 Age: 22 Bats: L Throws: L Height: 6'2" Weight: 215
Origin: Round 1, 2016 Draft (#35 overall)

The Report: I'll be honest at the outset and admit that I don't know if our staff looks this year really justify holding the line to this extent on Trammell. A year ago we filed him as a potential plus hit/plus power center fielder and ranked him as the 11th-best prospect in baseball despite the top-line performance being merely okay. He was internally divisive even then, and reports on his swing went backwards during his time with the Reds in 2019. Despite the swing issues, the underlying hit tool remains intact, with plus bat speed and good feel for the barrel. The approach is still a bit raw even after three full professional seasons focusing solely on baseball, and he often prioritizes contact over getting his raw power into games. The plus raw power is still there and will flash. The athleticism is unquestioned, he's a plus runner with excellent body control with the closing speed for center, but his present outfield instincts might limit him to a corner, likely left since his arm strength is fringy at best.

Trammell is in some ways both high variance and low. The baseline offensive and defensive skills for a solid fourth outfielder are here, so there's not a ton of downside risk in the profile. I can't help but think there is still a switch to be flipped, and he'll end up a plus regular for a few years. It's getting harder and harder to see it though, but sometimes you stay on a guy for an extra year just in case.

Variance: Medium. The hit tool and athleticism will likely get him a major league role, but he's never really gotten his plus raw power into games and might end up in left field.

Mark Barry's Fantasy Take: It's hard to look at Trammell's progress in 2018 and not think last season was somewhat of a disappointment. He struck out more, was inefficient in his base thievery, and hit .234 in 514 trips to the plate across two organizations. Still, despite a turbulent year for the 22-year-old, sometimes you just need to bet on the skills and underlying tools. Trammell still got on base at a nice clip, and the athleticism that we loved heading into last season is certainly still there. Maybe he slides a couple of spots on the dynasty-101, but he shouldn't plummet.

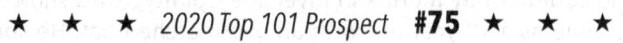

★ ★ ★ *2020 Top 101 Prospect* **#75** ★ ★ ★

6

Adrian Morejon   LHP   OFP: 60   ETA: 2019
Born: 02/27/99   Age: 21   Bats: L   Throws: L   Height: 6'0"   Weight: 175
Origin: International Free Agent, 2016

The Report: In just about any other system save for a couple, Morejon is probably the top pitching prospect and a definite top-fiver. He made his major league debut at 20 this year, after all. AJ Preller and company, however, have tapped into some sort of arcane sorcery, evil or otherwise, that blesses the south tip of the Golden Coast with enough young talent that Morejon falls just outside those tiers for San Diego. He's a three-pitch pitcher with two at-least above-average pitches and the third with the potential to join them. Morejon's fastball sat 92-94 for most of the year, and he ticked it up to 96 (t98) in short big-league bursts. He commands the pitch well and gets aggressive with it early in counts to draw contact. That plan of attack worked well in the Texas League, not so much above it. He pairs the gas with a harder changeup at 83-86 that has a good amount of drop, and a curveball at 79-81. The breaker has an inconsistent shape, but when it's on it works 12-5 in a hurry to generate swings and misses.

He doesn't always repeat the delivery efficiently, and his arm was really dragging over the summer, leading to a stressed shoulder and forcing an early shutdown in August. The talent has never been Morejon's problem, but a tricep injury cost him a chunk of 2017 and he managed just 44 innings last season before looking reasonably healthy in a brief AFL cameo. Durability will drive the role, there's a higher bullpen risk now.

Variance: Higher than ideal for an already-debuted prospect. A healthy Morejon is going to be good at something in the majors, the question is what. At his highest ceiling he could be a high No. 3 starter, though command and health questions cloud that path significantly.

Mark Barry's Fantasy Take: We all know that pitching prospects are health risks, and Morejon especially has battled nagging injuries for the better part of his career. But I can't help but think now is a decent time to buy low on the lefty, who seems to be buried in this system by buzzier guys. Morejon struck dudes out at every level, including a five-game stint in the big leagues (just don't look at the ERA), and still has a starter's profile despite debuting from the bullpen. He's got SP2-3 upside, but you know, injuries and stuff.

───────── ★ ★ ★ *2020 Top 101 Prospect* **#94** ★ ★ ★ ─────────

7 Gabriel Arias   SS   OFP: 60   ETA: Late 2021
Born: 02/27/00   Age: 20   Bats: R   Throws: R   Height: 6'1"   Weight: 201
Origin: International Free Agent, 2016

The Report: The third of many 2016 J2 alums dotting this list, and one of almost as many who couldn't buy a drink in Riverside County, Arias showed up to the California League as a 19-year-old with an overmatched bat. He spent the first couple months fishing at every predictable piece of spin he saw, and he saw a lot of it. That turned out to be a good thing in the long run, as he made some nice strides in advancing his approach and becoming more disciplined around the zone as the year went on. It's the second straight season he's made successful in-season adjustments across a full season.

Arias is a strong, physical kid with excellent hand speed that shows up on both sides of the ball. The glove is sweet at the six, with a baseline fluidity to his movements that allows for quick reactions and a graceful attack on the ball. He's not especially fast, but his movements are quick and efficient, and he anticipates his contact points very well. It's at least a plus arm, and he controls his body consistently well into his throws.

Even with the strides he made in the box, he's still an aggressive swinger in the zone, and he'll get himself out on pitchers' pitches early in counts. He generates solid bat speed, and there's above-average raw power that he's shown an ability to find in games once he settles in to his league.

Variance: Moderately high; he's going to be a very good defender at shortstop with at least some offensive utility, so the floor here is high. But so is the range in value between a first-division shortstop and, like, 2016 Zack Cozart.

Mark Barry's Fantasy Take: Oh cool, a defense-first prospect that learned how to hit and now could be really good. This system just keeps on giving. Arias doesn't walk and still strikes out more than you'd like, but his breakout 2019 probably puts him in the top-200ish for dynasty prospects.

8. Michel Baez   RHP
OFP: 55 **ETA:** 2019
Born: 01/21/96 Age: 24 Bats: R Throws: R Height: 6'8" Weight: 220
Origin: International Free Agent, 2016

The Report: Part of the Padres' heralded 2016 international haul, Baez pitched professionally in Cuba before signing with San Diego as a 20-year-old. The 6-foot-8 monster pitched exclusively as a starter in his first two minor league seasons, but after missing seven weeks with shoulder inflammation to begin the 2019 season, Baez worked out of the bullpen at Double-A Amarillo, where he dominated and earned a promotion to the big leagues in late July.

The right-hander maintains an efficient and athletic delivery despite his size, allowing him to adequately command his 96-98 mph fastball. A promising 85-87 mph changeup has been effective at the big league level, separating nicely from the high-90s heat. Baez has utilized an above-average-flashing 84-86 mph slider as his primary breaker in the past, though he consolidated to an occasional 76-79 mph curveball to round out his bullpen repertoire last year.

Baez proved generally effective in his first work out of the big league bullpen last season, but the Padres plan to return him to the rotation next spring, where he'll be part of a deep stable of young, exciting arms competing for big league innings. As his teammate Chris Paddack proved last season, a quality fastball-changeup combo can be a great foundation, but Baez will have to further groom his breaking-balls, if he's to last deep into ballgames and hang onto a coveted rotation spot.

Variance: Moderate; he showed the stuff can get big leaguers out last year, but health and role questions still swirl.

Mark Barry's Fantasy Take: The Padres are treating Baez as a starter, which makes sense, but I'd have a hard time envisioning the big guy holding up after spending the entirety of the 2019 campaign using the bullpen cart. He could be a stud closer, but relying on a prospect as closer-in-waiting is a little like rolling the dice on sun-baked potato salad (read: bad, it's bad).

9. Tirso Ornelas   OF
OFP: 55 **ETA:** 2022
Born: 03/11/00 Age: 20 Bats: L Throws: R Height: 6'3" Weight: 200
Origin: International Free Agent, 2017

The Report: The 19-year-old corner outfielder appeared overwhelmed during much of the 2019 California League season, scuffling to a .203 batting average before being reassigned to Arizona's development league to regain some confidence. That didn't really work, either, at least in terms of his production, as he continued to struggle mightily in the box in Arizona. He picked it up after returning to Lake Elsinore in August, hitting .280 with eight extra-base hits down the stretch, but it was a tough year pretty much start to finish.

Ornelas is an impressive physical specimen with plenty of natural strength and power, though neither his current swing nor his approach generates much lift or backspin at all. His coordination and bat-to-ball ability are among his strengths, and he's patient at times to a fault right now. He's currently at his best with a middle-of-the-field hitting approach, though eventually he's going to have to start to learn how to get more aggressive in hitting counts and turn on pitches with some semblance of authority. For now, in-game power production remains very much a figment of our collective imagination. Ornelas runs well for his size and has good mobility in the outfield, even making four starts in center field last season. His strong and accurate throwing arm is best-suited for right, however, where he could be an above-average defender.

It's an impressive collection of extremely raw tools, and the eventual package can be that of an all-around corner outfielder with a plus hit tool and above-average power potential, even if the tool and role grades remain entirely projection at this stage.

Variance: Extreme; last season's struggles seemed to affect his confidence at times, and there's just an enormous gulf between his present and potential future selves.

Mark Barry's Fantasy Take: A guy that doesn't run, get to power in games or hit for average? Where do I sign up? Admittedly that's a little mean to Ornelas, but the 19-year-old is almost 100 percent projection right now, and needs to take a slight step in the right direction in any of these areas before I'd feel good about rostering him.

10 Ryan Weathers   LHP   OFP: 55   ETA: 2022
Born: 12/17/99   Age: 20   Bats: R   Throws: L   Height: 6'1"   Weight: 230
Origin: Round 1, 2018 Draft (#7 overall)

The Report: Weathers is a slightly shorter, wider, left-handed clone of his father, which is a thing to be. The body type and arm action are real mirrors, with junior taking a quick, short arm stroke that makes his pitches jump on hitters. He burst out of the gate in the Midwest League to rule April, but he never really looked quite right after that, laboring through outings with flagging velocity.

He's a very good athlete, with major league bloodlines and a state basketball championship on his resume, and the stuff is very good, too. Healthy Weathers rolls 94-95 with that aforementioned jump, a product of tight spin and ride, and he'll work in a curve and change that both grade out as solid complements. He's shown the ability to execute sequencing with all three, and the compact delivery gives him consistency and command. You can see why the club drafted him where they did.

He hasn't developed any dominant finishing pitches yet, and the arm slot limits his options for creating new ones. But he can thrive off and around enough barrels to be a highly effective rotation member with his current arsenal.

Variance: High; there's a good amount of pedigree here, but prep arms are prep arms, and balky shoulders don't know anyone's bonus number.

Mark Barry's Fantasy Take: Weathers seems like a pretty safe bet for a pretty safe pitcher, but the middling strikeout numbers and injury history produce real questions about his ultimate upside. I'd keep him on the radar in leagues with 250-300 prospects..

The Next Ten

11 Tucupita Marcano INF
Born: 09/16/99 Age: 20 Bats: L Throws: R Height: 6'0" Weight: 170
Origin: International Free Agent, 2016

Marcano's named for his home, and after signing with the Padres in 2016 for $320,000 the Tucupita, Venezuela native made his way stateside in 2018. He spent the entirety of the 2019 regular season in the Midwest League before being promoted to High-A for a postseason run, and thus finished the year as yet another 19-year-old in Lake Elsinore. Marcano inspires comps to former system-mate Luis Urias, as their skill sets are nearly identical. Marcano is a plus athlete with a plus hit tool, and he shows advanced skills as a smooth defender at second base. The club has worked him in at short and third as well, but while his reactions and hands can play at either spot, the arm's light for the left side. He's very thin at present, and will need to develop physically, but even with added strength the power potential will be limited if the bat path remains flat. He's fun to watch and a really intelligent player in all facets of the game, which yields a higher degree of confidence in the growth and development to come. If Marcano were a part of any other organization he would be a slam dunk top-10 prospect, but alas, even his 80-grade name wasn't enough to push him over the hump here in this crazy-deep system.

12 Owen Miller INF
Born: 11/15/96 Age: 23 Bats: R Throws: R Height: 6'0" Weight: 190
Origin: Round 3, 2018 Draft (#84 overall)

IThe club's third-rounder in 2018, Miller skipped High-A last year and jumped straight from the Midwest League to Texas. He looked no worse for the wear after the aggressive promotion, posting an above-average offensive season while adding up-the-middle defensive value at second and short. The offensive package is solid all around, as he pairs above-average bat speed with a good feel to hit. He understands the zone well and attacks strikes, and while it's below-average raw he should be able to bring a modest amount of pop into games. He moves well at short, turning plus speed into solid range, though the arm is borderline for the left side. It's a solid utility profile, and he has the athleticism and baseball IQ to potentially add some outfield into the mix to further bolster his chances of impacting a 25-man roster down the line.

13 Jeisson Rosario   CF
Born: 10/22/99   Age: 20   Bats: L   Throws: L   Height: 6'1"   Weight: 191
Origin: International Free Agent, 2016

Yes, he too was in the 2016 haul, and the Dominican is a plus-defending outfielder with exceptional athleticism. Playing as a 19-year-old in High-A last season, Rosario led the California League with 87 walks, though the patience came at a cost, as the deep counts he routinely worked resulted in a lot of hittable pitches passing by and sub-optimal contact quality. His is a lean wiry strength, and while he'll show occasional gap power, he rarely seeks to drive the ball and most of his extra-base hits are the product of his plus-or-better speed. He shows some baseline aptitude for swiping bags, and positive baserunning value should be a part of his game. Rosario possesses the arm strength to play right field, but his expansive range and predatorial closing speed are best utilized in center, where he's capable of growing into a true plus defender. While the hit tool looks like it may be a slower burn in refinement, Rosario's blend of dynamic play-making and graceful athleticism gives him a lot to build on and should afford him all the time he needs to round into a valuable player.

14 Edward Olivares   CF
Born: 03/06/96   Age: 24   Bats: R   Throws: R   Height: 6'2"   Weight: 186
Origin: International Free Agent, 2014

Olivares is one of the poster children for the depth of this system. A year after cracking our top 20 as a physical toolsy guy, he went out and put up a 114 DRC+ in the Texas League while improving offensively pretty much across the board at a higher level, and he only managed to nudge his way up a half-dozen spots on the list. He's started to grow into some of the physical projection he's long threatened, and it wasn't a fluke that a bunch of his doubles and triples turned into homers. There's some inconsistency in the barrel delivery still, but he's continued to make a bunch of contact against better arms. He's gained a bit of explosiveness to his stride with added strength, and, provided he continues to hone his route-running, he can become a value-adding center fielder. He'll be 24 this year with a full, successful season at Double-A under his belt, and he should factor into the mix for big-league at-bats at some point in 2020.

15 Ronald Bolaños   RHP
Born: 08/23/96   Age: 23   Bats: R   Throws: R   Height: 6'3"   Weight: 220
Origin: International Free Agent, 2016

Bolaños is the eighth and final member of San Diego's 2016 J2 crew to crack our top 15, and his arm is as electric as any name above or below him. He's a big, physical right-hander who has grown a bunch since his days as Michel Baez's teammate in Cuba. His big-league debut last year came shortly before he turned 23 and was earned largely on the back of an excellent fastball that sits mid 90s and will touch 98. He generates plenty of life and ride with the pitch crossfiring from a three-quarters slot, though his fine command of the pitch is below-average, as his arm will show up late and sail balls arm-side. Behind the fastball is a kitchen sink full of a slider with flashes of two-plane action, a show-me change, and a deep curveball he'll throw whenever and mess around with the velocity and trajectory. The delivery is aggressive and up-tempo, and he'll rush through checkpoints and get out of sync. Fringy command and control will make him less consistent as a rotation option, but he can fill starts and log multiple middle innings a pop in 2020.

16 Reggie Lawson   RHP
Born: 08/02/97   Age: 22   Bats: R   Throws: R   Height: 6'4"   Weight: 205
Origin: Round 2, 2016 Draft (#71 overall)

It's easy to lose Lawson in the depth of the Padres' system after he was limited to just six starts last year, but he's still just 22 years old and showed flashes in the Arizona Fall League of the talent that prompted San Diego to select him 71st-overall in 2016. The fastball sits in the mid 90s with life, and he complements it well with a curve that generates plenty of swing-and-miss. The changeup is not as advanced, but it does show promise of eventually turning into an average pitch. Prior to injuring his elbow last spring there were times the control would waver, but the delivery is easy and he's athletic enough to eventually clean up some of those issues. If he can stay healthy, the stuff is there for Lawson to eventually sneak his way onto the back of the rotation, and there's a healthy fallback route where he cranks up the heat in short bursts to evolve into a lights-out reliever.

17 Hudson Potts   3B
Born: 10/28/98   Age: 21   Bats: R   Throws: R   Height: 6'3"   Weight: 205
Origin: Round 1, 2016 Draft (#24 overall)

One of the things they teach us here when we're brand new members of the BP prospect team is an important axiom: "Someone is paying this person to play professional baseball; it's up to you to figure out why." Potts is one of the prospects that tested this axiom in 2019. The 2016 first-rounder from Southlake, Texas was quite young for the level at 20, and he showed power with 17 homers. But they came at an expensive cost of poor patience and a lot of swing-and-miss, and he was frequently overmatched at the level. The glove at the hot corner stalled some, and now looks more okay than great, so the bat needs to do a good bit of work to drive the profile. We'll chalk this year up to a young player in over his head against much more advanced competition, and see if he can't answer us the original question a little more clearly in what figures to be a repeat engagement at Amarillo.

18 Joey Cantillo LHP
Born: 12/18/99   Age: 20   Bats: L   Throws: L   Height: 6'4"   Weight: 220
Origin: Round 16, 2017 Draft (#468 overall)

Many pitchers in the Midwest League had better stuff, but none dominated hitters the way that Cantillo did last season. The former 16th-round selection struck out 128 in just 98 innings and held opposing hitters to a .173 average. The arsenal is underwhelming on the surface, with a fastball that sits in the mid to upper 80s and a big, soft curve, but he gets the job done with feel and deception. The changeup is the best secondary; it looks like the fastball out of his hand and he's confident enough to throw it in any situation. He gets good downhill plane and some velocity will come as he physically matures, but there will always be a dependence on pitchability. It will be interesting to see how that profile fares against the more hitter-friendly stops in the upper minors.

19 Blake Hunt C
Born: 11/10/98   Age: 21   Bats: R   Throws: R   Height: 6'3"   Weight: 215
Origin: Round 2, 2017 Draft (#69 overall)

The Padres saw a future above-average defender with a bit of pop when they went overslot to lure Hunt away from a Pepperdine commitment in 2017. He hasn't disappointed behind the dish since signing, blocking well and showing quality lateral movement for someone his size. He's also tough to run on, as he is quick to transfer and has a strong, accurate arm. Offensively, he's still a work in progress. The bat speed is average and there's length to the swing, though he does control the zone well. Fringe-average power should eventually play in-game, mostly based on his raw strength. There's still a ways to go for the bat, but Hunt's strong defense will give him plenty of opportunity to figure it out, and should eventually lead him to a sustained big-league role.

20 Hudson Head CF
Born: 04/08/01   Age: 19   Bats: L   Throws: L   Height: 6'1"   Weight: 180
Origin: Round 3, 2019 Draft (#84 overall)

Head popped up last spring as a late-rising Texas prep bat, and San Diego made an aggressive play for him, grabbing him in the third round and signing him for the slot value of the 23rd-overall pick in the draft to buy him out of a strong commitment to Oklahoma. He's a five-tool player with just the kind of projectable frame to support such a towering draft commitment. He's thin and wiry at present, and while he's never going to grow into a ton of bulk, there's ample room to add lean muscle and pack on strength. There's an arm bar and some rigidity to the present load, but the swing is fluid on trigger, with quality bat speed and whip. He generates excellent extension and already gets into his legs well, which bodes well for his ability to grow into raw power that should reach at least above-average, with the potential for a tick more depending on how full he fills out. He's an efficient runner with a gliding gait, and the speed translates pretty well in the outfield already. It's not a no-doubt center field profile, but the raw fundamentals are there, and when all's said and done he could very well wind up with above-average tools all the way across the board. Given how aggressive the org is, he's likely to see plenty of full-season reps next season and could move up this list right quick.

Personal Cheeseball

PC **Eguy Rosario** INF
Born: 08/25/99 Age: 20 Bats: R Throws: R Height: 5'9" Weight: 150
Origin: International Free Agent, 2015

Contrary to what I wrote in my Eyewitness Report on Rosario, it turned out that he wasn't Rule 5-eligible this winter after all. Hence he'll benefit from another year of development without needing to be on anyone's 40-Man roster. On the dirt, he displays enough glove, arm, and athleticism to handle all three infield positions to the left of first base. At the plate, he combines above-average bat-to-ball skills with advanced discipline, though he struggles to catch up with plus stuff. At present, he hits the majority of his batted balls on the ground, but his strong lower half implies that the game power could play up to below-average if he learns how to lift the ball without sacrificing too much contact. The likely outcome is a fifth infielder rounding out a first-division roster, but there's a chance he'll grow into a full-time player. Despite having spent each of the last two seasons in High-A, he only turned 20 in late August. Eguy (pronounced egg-y) is well-cooked beyond his age, and salmonella-free! (editing note: Wilson, don't you dare cut the last pun out).

Low Minors Sleeper

LMS **Joshua Mears** OF
Born: 02/21/01 Age: 19 Bats: R Throws: R Height: 6'3" Weight: 230
Origin: Round 2, 2019 Draft (#48 overall)

It's not cheating to take last summer's second-rounder in this slot, because in most other systems he'd probably crack the top 20 on pedigree alone. He was an underslot pick to clear space for Head, but he's a sight to behold all the same. He's an enormous kid, standing 6-foot-3 and 230 as an 18-year-old on draft day, and there is corresponding strength for days. There is also a corresponding sluggishness to his swing progression right now. The hands drift forward off a shallow load to choke off some of his torque, and he got eaten alive by velocity after signing, whiffing more than 30-percent of the time in the AZL. The raw power is sick, though, and the frame could tighten and grow into elite full-body strength. He runs well for his size, and showed good instincts on the bases as well as some tracking ability in right. It's not the highest-probability profile, but it's a fun bat to dream on actualizing down the line.

Top Talents 25 and Under (as of 4/1/2020)

1. Fernando Tatis, Jr.
2. Chris Paddack
3. MacKenzie Gore
4. Luis Patiño
5. CJ Abrams
6. Francisco Mejia
7. Luis Campusano
8. Taylor Trammell
9. Cal Quantrill
10. Adrian Morejon

A pulled hammy put Tatito on the shelf in May, and then a back injury ultimately ended his season in the middle of August, and those were both huge bummers because it sure was a lot of fun to watch him play in between those extended absences. The list of 20-year-olds to put up three-and-a-half win seasons is a real short one, and while his offensive production surely punched above its weight – .410 BABIPs and 30-percent strikeout rates don't tend to be all that sustainable – we can forgive those shortcomings some since, you know, the whole he's-20-years-old thing. He's a franchise cornerstone player in an organization that appears flush with those sorts.

On the other side of the ball, Chris Paddack sure did look like a front-of-the-rotation starter for an organization that also, somehow, appears flush with those sorts. The 23-year-old's four-WARP debut was by and large the sustainable-looking kind according to his under-the-hood metrics, though the arsenal's probably going to need more refinement if he's going to stay in that rarefied air. He's fastball-heavy, which is just a fine thing to be in light of his fastball being very, very good, but hitters started making a bit more contact against his cambio as the season progressed, and he's still not great at spinning the ball. He's very good, though, and should help anchor a resurgent rotation for the first half of the decade to come.

Francisco Mejia continued to remind everyone that catcher development isn't linear, but he flashed a bunch of reasons for optimism that his is progressing solidly in the right direction. The bat slogged early, but it warmed up late with glimpses of a long-heralded plus hit tool, and the glove true to form, performed okay enough behind the dish. It remains an offense-first profile that yangs nicely with Hedges' glovely yin, and another step forward in the box next year in his age-24 season can check a big box for the franchise.

Paul Quantrill's son hasn't quite fulfilled the lofty expectations that come with a top-ten draft pedigree, but his big-league debut last year was absolutely fine. There were some warning signs, however, notably that his vaunted changeup didn't actually fool hitters nearly as much as he needs it to, and after an initial bout of effectiveness his slider missed fewer and fewer bats as the season progressed and hitters adjusted. But hey, if a true No. 4 starter's the 10th guy on your organization's 25U list you're in pretty good shape, and that's where it appears things are right now in San Diego.

Beyond the top 10 here there's also a deep trove of useful pieces for good measure; it's unclear what exactly we should expect from Manuel Margot going forward after another sub-one WARP season in more or less full playing time, but there are still fun underlying skills and sometimes guys like him'll pop a few years into their careers. Josh Naylor flashed some of the barrel skills that got him drafted at the top of a first round, along with a good chunk of his defensive deficiencies, and Andrés Muñoz breathed enough fire in his debut to inspire confidence that the club is deep in the process of developing yet another back-of-the-bullpen stalwart to complement its embarrassing riches of forthcoming starting pitching.

All of this is to confirm that after years of terrible, terrible big-league play, San Diego has triangulated an awfully exciting young core that should finally be able to give their neighbors to the north a run for their NL West money in the 2020s.

Part 3: Featured Articles

The Baseball Is Juiced (Again)

Robert Arthur

This article originally appeared at Baseball Prospectus on April 5, 2019.

It started when the normally reliable Chris Sale got lit up for three homers by the Mariners in the Red Sox's season opener. It was part of a record number of taters that flew on Opening Day, as starters from Sale to Zack Greinke were taken deep by the handful. Then Christian Yelich hit a home run in each of his first four games, tying yet another MLB record, this one for consecutive games with a dinger to start a season.

It didn't take long for fans and players to begin whispering and tweeting about the baseballs being juiced again. It's early yet for us to come to any definitive conclusion about the 2019 season, but preliminary data shows that the baseball has returned to its aerodynamic peak. Whether that means this season will smash home run records like 2017 did remains to be seen.

Before home run explosion over the last few years, no one worried too much about the baseball's air resistance. While MLB and Rawlings (the company that manufactures the official baseballs) kept track of dozens of metrics to make sure that the ball was consistent from month to month, they didn't measure drag.

But drag is incredibly important in determining how likely a hitter is to knock one out of the park. As baseballs become more aerodynamic, they travel further given a certain initial velocity. A deep fly ball that might have been caught at the warning track can instead go into the first row of the stands. A three percent change in drag coefficient can work to add about five feet to a well-hit fly ball, which can in turn increase home runs league wide by an astounding 10-15 percent.

It's possible to measure the aerodynamics of the baseball using the pitch-tracking radars currently in place in each MLB ballpark. By calculating the loss of speed from when the pitch is released to when it crosses the plate, you can directly measure the drag coefficient on the baseball. I first wrote about the role of decreasing drag in boosting home runs in 2017, and MLB's commission of scientists and statisticians later confirmed that the more aerodynamic baseballs in use that year were largely to blame for the spike in home runs. The same commission rejected some alternate hypotheses, like rising temperatures and a league-wide boost in launch angle pushing more balls over the fence.

The current era has featured some large fluctuations in drag coefficient, leading to first an explosion in 2016 and 2017, and then a dialing back of homers last year. Curious about the record-breaking home run tallies in the last few days, I used the same methodology to measure the aerodynamics of the baseballs so far in 2019.

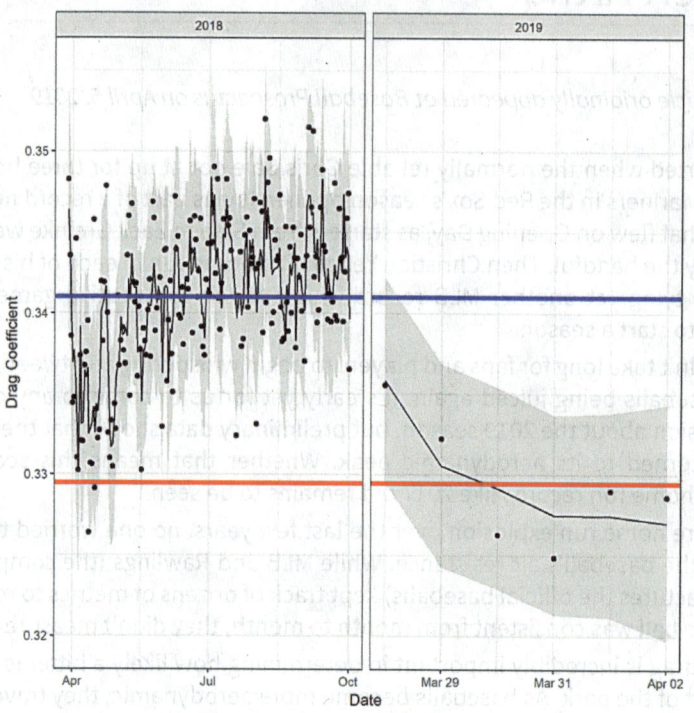

We're only a week into the 2019 season, but the drag numbers so far are among the lowest recorded in the last calendar year. With apologies for gory math, the current 2019 season average drag coefficient (the red line) would be below the 95 percent credible interval (the shaded area) for about nine-tenths of the 2018 season. (I used a Bayesian Random Walk model implemented in INLA to calculate these credible intervals, averaging the drag numbers in each game and adjusting for park.)

There were only a handful of six-day stretches in 2018 that had drag numbers below what we're seeing now, and most were in late June and early July. All of this means that 2019's data so far is quite a bit different than what we saw through most of last year.

These drag coefficients factor out the effects of temperature and air density, so they aren't a product of April cold. However, the numbers could be deceptive if the radars used to track pitches have changed from year to year. I consulted with some experts within baseball who were not aware of any specific modifications to the radar this year that could produce this pattern, but it's an important caveat of which to be aware.

On the one hand, it's only been six days, and we don't quite have the statistical basis to say that these drag coefficients are unprecedented compared to 2018. On the other hand, we've witnessed about 5,000 fastballs so far this season, so it's not as if our sample size is small. At least so far, the baseball has played like it's much more aerodynamic than it was last year. In fact, the current drag coefficient is really only comparable to 2017, when the baseballs were more aerodynamic than they had been in at least a decade.

It's not just fancy radar tracking indicating that the baseball is flying through the air more easily. The current number of home runs per game (as of this writing) is the highest it's been since the heady days of 2017, the year that teams and players broke dinger-related records everywhere you looked. That's especially remarkable considering that we're in what is typically the coldest part of the regular season, when lower temperatures and higher winds tend to suppress offense and keep balls in the air within the park. Comparing only from April to April, this year's rate of home runs per fly ball is even a little bit higher than it was in 2017.

With that said, the current measurements are no guarantee that 2019 will be another year of record-shattering homer hitting. The trouble with the drag measurements is that they are not consistent from June to August, from week to week, or even sometimes from day to day. Whether because of natural manufacturing variation or differences in the underlying supplies of cowhide and thread that go into the baseballs, drag has a tendency to fluctuate up and down over the course of a year. So the homers that fly in the first week of April wouldn't necessarily clear the fence a week later.

It's possible that this one-week drop in drag coefficient subsides and the baseball returns to its 2018 levels. On the other hand, it's almost equally probable that the ball becomes even more slippery and flies ever farther. Either way, it's clear that the baseball's air resistance is something to keep an eye on for the remainder of the 2019 season.

—*Robert Arthur is an author of Baseball Prospectus.*

The Moral Hazard of Playing It Safe

Craig Goldstein

This article originally appeared at Baseball Prospectus on August 6, 2019.

A couple days prior to the trade deadline, amidst a sea of tranquility posing as the lead up to the trade deadline, Bob Nightengale took to Twitter. Nightengale, who was probably wearing his pants backwards at the time, tweeted that MLB GMs were coming around on the idea that the unified trade deadline should be moved back from July 31 to August 15, so they could better assess their positions in the standings and whether they should buy or sell. To which I said:

This might strike some as reductive and churlish. And it might be that, but it isn't really wrong, either. Jeff Quinton wrote a great piece discussing the environmental factors that enable front offices to avoid risk without upsetting the apple cart within their own fanbases. I don't believe that it goes far enough, however. His article gives us the proper framework through which to understand why these behaviors have been allowed to seep into front offices throughout the league. Understanding the reasons behind these actions are different from excusing them, though, and GMs should not be let off the hook for their non-competitive approach to the trade deadline (much less the offseason).

⚾ ⚾ ⚾

It's fair to say that fans as a group have rarely, if ever, been pro-player. It is also fair to say that in the time during and following the Moneyball revolution, the pendulum swung from fans who cared intensely about winning in the moment (and thus might be intolerant of a rebuilding approach) to fans who supported building a team that could compete throughout multiple seasons, viewing the playoffs as a crapshoot, with the thought that getting multiple bites at the apple was a better approach than taking a bigger bite in any one season.

There's nothing wrong with that approach, and I still find merit in that argument. However, it seems that the pendulum has swung too far in that direction. Teams are overvaluing some of the individual factors that make themselves long-term contenders rather than attempting to seize a championship when given the opportunity. It's a difficult needle to thread.

And surely, they (and those in similar positions) would have liked another two weeks to clarify where they stand so as to better marshal their resources. We've all asked for a few more minutes when staring at a menu. But all of these GMs and front office personnel are where they are to make difficult decisions. They have proprietary data and internal analysts dedicated to understanding their position relative to the rest of the league, and how any move in the here and now impacts their long-term vision. To complain (if that report is accurate) that over half the season is not enough to properly assess their season is bullshit of the highest order. Move the deadline, and you'd simply have increasingly discounted trade offers because teams would be acquiring even less control of anyone they're acquiring, rental or not.

Major league front offices are behaving like the managers they lampooned two decades ago. They're effectively sacrificing a runner to second in the ninth inning—not because it's the correct move, but rather because it is safe. It used to be that the phrase "moral hazard" was used to describe general managers who made ill-fated, short-sighted decisions aimed at locking in wins and securing their jobs at the expense of their team's future. Now, general managers are guilty of committing moral hazards in the opposite direction, playing it utterly safe and terrified of becoming scapegoats.

In lieu of bold action, they opt to pussyfoot around a current window of contention, choosing instead to play the long game and stack up years of control like they're blocks in a game of Jenga. GMs pass on signing quality players in free agency because the back-end of the deal might look bad, and because they might be able to squeeze out 70 percent of the production from a player who costs a tenth as much. That's a safer investment, too, because it's also hard to prove a negative—it's impossible to prove that Manny Machado would make the Mets a playoff team in 2019-2020, but it's easy to say that the back half of Robinson Cano's contract sucks. Owners, who rule over GM's jobs, are also humans with human brain processes that will always make the so-called albatross contract uglier than the road not taken.

These days, GMs are remembered for the bad deals they make and the surplus value they generate, not the acquisition of expensive, necessary talents that meet their market worth (or fall slightly short while still providing significant on-field value). And front offices know that one or two expensive misfires can cost them their jobs, no matter how many good deals they make.

No front office exemplifies this ethos more than the Toronto Blue Jays. General Manager Ross Atkins had this to say following the Blue Jays underwhelming trade deadline:

This is by no means the first time that an executive will cite years of control to justify their actions, which is often just another way of saying "don't look at what we got, look at how much we got of it." Atkins touts quantity to elide the discussion of quality—either, that of the players acquired, or those given up. Remember: the other teams presumably value years of control, too.

Atkins also had some thoughts to offer regarding free agents back in early 2018:

This ignores, of course, whether the player can create enough value in the front end of a contract to justify the longer term of a deal, and the decline that often occurs in the back end. It also ignores whether the player can fill a need the team requires and put them in a position to compete for and win a championship. But as teams seemingly avoid contention at all, where they might end up having to consider and later justify some of these tough decisions, we still see risk-averse approaches.

Anthony Fenech's article on two trades that recently extended GM Al Avila didn't make got at this issue rather well:

> Passing on those deals was defensible: Both players had yet to break out and trading [Michael] Fulmer—a pitcher who appeared to be a future ace, no matter his injury concerns—would have taken serious gumption, opening Avila up to strong criticism.

Avoiding strong criticism is something each of us can understand as a motivation, but the avoidance of criticism only matters if that criticism is valid. In Fulmer's case, shoving his injury concerns aside affects not only the years that the team controls him (he is currently missing a full season due to Tommy John surgery) but also the quality of those seasons, as his knee and elbow injuries combined to dampen his effectiveness even when healthy enough to pitch. But it was easy to present the then-current image of Fulmer as a top of the rotation pitcher who the team had under its domain for the next five seasons as something to build around. The status quo isn't nearly as often second-guessed as a decision that disrupts it.

⚾   ⚾   ⚾

MLB GMs are risk-averse to a fault. They are ivy-educated and consulting firm-approved, and yet they can't seem to avoid leaving wins on the table in their all-consuming lust for a non-existent $/WAR championship. They are supposed to zig when everyone else zags, and not merely pay lip service to the idea of zigging through a calculated PR plan built on convincing the fan base their approach is novel when it actually apes most of their competitors. Instead they've become far more concerned with making safe, accepted-by-the-new-common-wisdom decisions, such that our prior understanding of what a moral hazard is has become inverted.

I can't blame them entirely, and not only because of the reasons that Quinton illuminated in his article, but also because of the damage wrought by the introduction of the second wild card (WC2) spot. MLB's desire to have more teams in playoff contention has sparked anti-competitive behavior. Teams know now that they do not need to swing big as they assemble their roster because there is a good chance that a mediocre team can either catch fire and capture a division, or muddle along until they back into the WC2.

Simultaneously, the one-game playoff has neutered the WC1, putting an entire season on the flip of a coin like some sort of baseball-obsessed Anton Chigurh. While the one-game playoff makes sense as a way to increase the value of winning a division, it also means that if a front office doesn't like its chances of overcoming a behemoth like the Dodgers or Astros in the offseason, they have few incentives to chase glory. Similarly, the relative inaction in the NL Central at the trade deadline—despite a wide open division—can be explained by the idea that any high-variance investment could still result in only a wild card (or worse) result, given the mere two months left in the season to make an impact.

⚾ ⚾ ⚾

As stated at the top, we should not confuse reasons for excuses. The implementation of the second wild card is just one of many environmental factors that influence how each front office operates. I am convinced that it is one of the larger factors, but I am also convinced that organizations need to shed the yoke of "efficiency at all costs" so that they can instead pursue competition, as the spirit of the game intends. Until they do, we're all deadline losers.

—*Craig Goldstein is an author of Baseball Prospectus.*

Index of Names

Abrams, CJ 83, 102
Arias, Gabriel 96, 106
Avila, Pedro 98
Bachar, Lake 89
Baez, Michel 47, 107
Bednar, David 98
Bolanos, Ronald 98, 110
Campusano, Luis 84, 103
Cantillo, Joey 98, 112
Castillo, José 90
Cordero, Franchy 85
Cordoba, Allen 96
Cronenworth, Jake 96
Davies, Zach 49
Diaz, Miguel 91
Eickhoff, Jerad 51
France, Ty 20
Garcia, Greg 22
Gettys, Michael 96
Gore, MacKenzie 92, 101
Grisham, Trent 24
Guerra, Javy 93
Head, Hudson 96, 112
Hedges, Austin 26
Henry, Henry 98
Hosmer, Eric 28
Hunt, Blake 112
Kinsler, Ian 30
Lamet, Dinelson 53
Lawson, Reggie 98, 111
Loup, Aaron 98
Lucchesi, Joey 55
Machado, Manny 32
Marcano, Tucupita 96, 109
Mears, Joshua 113
Mejía, Francisco 34
Mejias-Brean, Seth 86
Miller, Owen 96, 109
Morejon, Adrian 94, 105
Munoz, Andres 57
Myers, Wil 37
Naylor, Josh 39
Nix, Jacob 98
Olivares, Edward 96, 110
Ona, Jorge 96
Ornelas, Tirso 96, 107
Paddack, Chris 59
Pagán, Emilio 61
Patino, Luis 95, 102
Perdomo, Luis 63
Pham, Tommy 41
Pomeranz, Drew 65
Potts, Hudson 96, 111
Powell, Boog 96
Profar, Jurickson 43
Quantrill, Cal 67
Quiroz, Esteban 96
Reed, Buddy 96
Reyes, Gerardo 69
Richards, Garrett 71
Rosario, Eguy 113
Rosario, Jeisson 96, 110

San Diego Padres 2020

Ruiz, Esteury 96	Van Gurp, Franklin 98
Stammen, Craig 73	Warren, Adam 77
Strahm, Matt 75	Weathers, Ryan 98, 108
Tatis Jr., Fernando 45	Wingenter, Trey 79
Torrens, Luis 87	Yacabonis, Jimmy 98
Trammell, Taylor 88, 104	Yates, Kirby 81